Playwrights for Tomorrow

VOLUME 7

EDITED, WITH AN INTRODUCTION, BY ARTHUR H. BALLET

PLAYWRIGHTS FOR TOMORROW

A Collection of Plays, Volume 7

THE UNIVERSITY OF MINNESOTA PRESS · MINNEAPOLIS

Printed in the United States of America at Lund Press, Minneapolis

Library of Congress Catalog Card Number: 66-19124
ISBN 0-8166-0579-3

PUBLISHED IN THE UNITED KINGDOM AND INDIA BY THE OXFORD UNIVERSITY PRESS, LONDON AND BOMBAY, AND IN CANADA BY THE COPP CLARK PUBLISHING CO. LIMITED, TORONTO

Playwrights for Tomorrow

VOLUME 7

INTRODUCTION

Arthur H. Ballet

I_N 1963 the Office for Advanced Drama Research (O.A.D.R.) was established at the University of Minnesota, with financial aid from the Rockefeller Foundation, its purpose being to provide an opportunity for playwrights to have new, experimental work performed in an atmosphere free from the pressures of the commercial theatre. Until 1969 productions supported by the O.A.D.R. were limited to the Minneapolis–St. Paul area, although its program has always drawn plays and writers from the entire country. With a renewed and expanded grant from the Rockefeller Foundation, the O.A.D.R. became national in its production activity, and its capability for underwriting productions was nearly doubled. The writers in this, the seventh, volume of *Playwrights for Tomorrow* represent the first full year of work with theatres in all parts of the country.

Unfortunately, not all the plays which were given developmental productions with aid from the O.A.D.R. can be published in this volume. James Damico's *The Trial of A. Lincoln* (premiered by the Hartford Stage Company), Charles Nolte's *The End of Ramadan* (by the Theatre in the Round Players, Minneapolis), David Freeman's *Captain Smith in His Glory* (by the Boston Theatre Company), Nathan Teitel's *The Initiation* (by the Seattle Repertory Company), Harding Lemay's *Death of Eagles* (by the University of Minnesota Theatre), Robert Campbell and Mervyn Murphy's *Parlor Game* (by the San Francisco State College Theatre), and Barry Litvack's *Honesty Is the Best Policy* (at the Cincinnati Playhouse in the Park) were all first produced under the aegis of the Office for Advanced Drama Research but cannot be included here.

Alexander Hierholzer, whose charming play *George and Grace and*

God was first produced in Alabama, is a full-time theatre manager. His assignment most recently has been with the Los Angeles production of *Hair*. A native of Richmond, Mr. Hierholzer has been a professional actor. This play was his first produced work for the theatre.

David Ball, who is the author of *Assassin!* produced by the Theatre in the Round Players, Minneapolis, is presently both a doctoral candidate in theatre and a playwriting intern at the Guthrie Theatre, also in Minneapolis. He is a prolific and a wide-ranging playwright and director. A number of his works have been produced elsewhere in the country.

Seymour Leichman, a well-known painter and author of children's stories, is a delightful exception among the contributors to the series. He will not take issue, I hope, when I say that he is not primarily a playwright. The play included here, *Freddie the Pigeon*, is the result of Cincinnati's Brooks Jones bringing together a fine director, Word Baker, and a fine artist, Leichman. The Playhouse in the Park and the streets of Cincinnati hosted the premiere of this unique work.

The Firehouse Theatre, late of Minneapolis and newly re-established in San Francisco, gave birth to Nancy Walter's *Rags*, which began as a poetic scenario, went through a metamorphosis as a dramatic exercise and improvisation by the company, and emerged as a major theatrical work; it eventually went to New York where it was played successfully at Cafe La Mama.

Stephen Grecco's *The Orientals* was first presented at his alma mater, Yale University's School of Drama. It represents an early and interesting work by a most promising writer who continues his graduate work.

Drive-In is yet another play which was first produced in Cincinnati, under Brooks Jones's direction. Its author, David Kranes, is a knowledgeable, experienced writer who presently teaches at the University of Utah. The play was one of the most hilarious ever presented by the Office for Advanced Drama Research.

Unproduced plays continue to flood the O.A.D.R. office. Each is read and considered and some — pathetically few — find their way to initial production with our help. For the most part, the production facilities are resident repertory theatres, but on occasion we work with quasi-professional and community as well as collegiate theatres. The search for new plays — and for theatres to do them — goes on.

Regrettably, American theatres and audiences have been led to great expectations — they expect ready-made, pre-packaged masterworks. The tendency is, too often, to refuse to take a chance on a play which may not yet be fully realized but which promises interesting plays to come, to decline to work with the playwright not yet approved by "the critics," and to give short shrift to plays which are unfamiliar and therefore somehow "unworthy."

Equally regrettable is the fact that of the thousands of plays which we've read to date, few have clear, individual voices. While the judgment of what will and what will not be included in our project must always be a subjective one, I think we lean — not to a "style" and not to a "kind" of play — but to a voice which quite clearly says, "This is what *I*'m saying and this is how *I*'m saying it." That first-person singular is what eventually makes a work of art stick.

Few of the plays are "great," and some of them perhaps may not even be "good." But they represent new writers with new ideas. They represent what living theatre is: individual voices with fresh approaches to *now*. Heidegger has suggested that the human condition ". . . is to be there." The writers in these volumes, and those omitted for various reasons, are — if nothing else — "there."

ALEXANDER HIERHOLZER

Grace and George and God

for Thomas and Michele
(of course)

Cast of Characters

GRACE

GEORGE

GOD

The Setting

At rise black lights reveal upstage many tall stylized flowers in bright luminescent colors, looking very innocently front. Offstage an organ plays "Bless This House" (in the style of Ethel Smith), and canaries sing brightly. The flowers slowly fade to the background as the general lighting rises, revealing up center the base of a large tree, rising far out of view. In the tree trunk, high above the stage level, is a Gothic cathedral window with stained glass of the same bright colors as the flowers. (At present the window is closed, unlighted, and unseen.) Down center, on its side, is a large pink and yellow egg resting on a nest of bright green plastic grass. The top quarter of the egg is hinged away from the audience.

A woman (Grace) and a man (George) are seated in the egg, facing each other. Only Grace's head, arms, and hands are visible. Her skin is pale green. She has short, neat hair, bangs, wears a large pink and blue Baby Snooks bow; she speaks with a nasal whine; her movements and speech suggest heaviness, sluggishness. George's bare skin, seen to his waist, is very white. He has thick, curly hair; his movements are clear, rapid, staccato.

As the action begins the lighting becomes bright and cheerful. The organ throughout — but softly — plays bouncy skating-rink-style tunes.

GRACE AND GEORGE AND GOD

GRACE

(*taking a lettuce leaf out of the basket and offering it to George*) Here, dear, eat this. It gives you strength and energy.

GEORGE

(*grabs it, eats*) Get off my back.

GRACE

(*holds out another leaf to him*) What did you say, dearest?

GEORGE

(*grabbing again*) Go to hell.

GRACE

You really must learn to properly chew your food, George. You never chew a thing. You gobble, gobble, gobble. That's very bad for your digestion, dear, and I'm sure it contributes to your elimination problem.

GEORGE

(*impatiently reaching for another leaf*) Shut up.

GRACE

George, I have a distinct feeling something is bothering you. (*He does not answer.*) George, dear, that's what a wife is for — to help you over your difficulties and share your experiences. How can I help if you won't share? (*He remains silent.*) Tell me, so we can talk to God about it.

GEORGE

(*reaching for another leaf*) That's a lot of shit.

GRACE

(*handing him the leaf*) I can't lightly toss aside my responsibilities as a helpmate, dear. (*He does not answer, but chews furiously.*) Come on now, tell Grace what's the matter.

GEORGE

You know damn well.

GRACE

(*handing him another leaf*) Oh, that again.

GEORGE

(*eating*) Yes . . *that*!

GRACE

You're too sensitive, George, too sensitive about a silly little thing that really doesn't matter. (*He chews furiously.*) Well, dear, you can't blame me.

GEORGE

Like hell I can't! You could adjust — if you wanted to.

GRACE

If *adjusting* is all that simple, why don't you do it?

GEORGE

It isn't easy for a man. How many times have I told you that?

GRACE

Well — I'll have you know it isn't easy for me either.

GEORGE

Don't be stupid. It doesn't mean as much to a woman. Everyone knows that.

GRACE

I don't know which quack did that survey, but he didn't ask me. I want you to know it means just as much to me as it does to you. (*She hands him more lettuce, then checks her shopping list.*) George, the next time you're near McGregor's pick up some French beans and radishes and parsley. They're really much better for you than this lettuce.

GEORGE

(*brooding*) It's emasculating.

GRACE

What's emasculating, dear?

GEORGE

(*purple with rage, shouting*) What the hell do you think we're talking about!

GRACE

Oh, that. To tell you the truth, I completely forget about it by the next morning.

GEORGE

(*shouting*) See! See! It doesn't mean a damn thing to you!

GRACE

(*handing him a carrot*) Have this nice carrot. Dr. Schlange says they're very good for the eyes. (*He greedily grabs the carrot, munches it happily; she swings her fingers in the grass, as one would do in the water from a rowboat; canaries chirp overhead.*) Did you notice the crocuses this morning? They're out again, and they're so lovely and fresh.

GEORGE

Fuck the crocuses.

GRACE

George, really. Suppose the children heard you.

GEORGE

So what. You don't give a damn who knows . . the other thing.

GRACE

George, you really exaggerate that. I don't know why you exaggerate everything, but you do, dear, you really do. You exaggerate.

GEORGE

How can you say I exaggerate, with that crowd standing there, cheering you on.

GRACE

I really don't know where they all come from. I don't invite anyone.

GEORGE

They sure know when to show up.

GRACE

(*hands him a lettuce leaf*) It is a little uncanny, isn't it, how they just appear out of the blue.

GEORGE

(*eating, but near tears*) They booed and hissed me, last time.

GRACE

I noticed that, dear, and I was very annoyed, I really was.

GEORGE

I'm surprised you noticed. You're always in such a state by then.

GRACE

Oh, I notice everything, George, I notice everything.

11

GEORGE

That proves it! It can't mean much to you if you notice everything. I'd be ten feet off the ground.

GRACE

Maybe that's the big difference between us, the basic difference between men and women. We just never lose control — over something like that. Regardless of how intense an experience may be, I never lose sight for one moment who I am and where I am.

GEORGE

(*very petulant*) It doesn't mean as much to you as it does to me.

GRACE

Well, at that moment it does. But if it did happen the other way around, George, it certainly wouldn't upset me the way it does you. There are so many other things in our relationship to build on.

GEORGE

(*sulking*) If you loved me you'd do something about it.

GRACE

George, dear, I can't tell you how many times I've discussed this with Dr. Schlange, and how many times I've taken the whole problem to God. In fact, I'm afraid I've worn her to a frazzle, listening to me talk about it. I do love you, you know I do, sweetheart, but I —

GEORGE

(*interrupting her*) Forget it. I'm through.

GRACE

(*cautiously*) What do you mean, George?

GEORGE

Just what I said. I'm through — it's all over.

GRACE

I can't believe my ears. I really can't believe my ears. You have to be joking. You can't mean that for one moment. We've been together too long for anything as silly as this to come between us. (*She takes a feather duster from inside the egg and nervously begins to dust.*)

GEORGE

It's not silly to me.

GRACE

If I live to be one hundred and fifty, I will never understand men. I cannot for the life of me understand how anyone as *intelligent* and *sensitive* and *attractive* as you are can possibly put so much importance in something as trivial as this. There's so much more to a relationship. We must make ourselves think of higher things. We have our home and our children and . .

and, and so much more, George. I refuse to believe for one moment that you are serious.

GEORGE

Well get it through your thick shell once and for all — I'm through.

GRACE

I'm grateful to God every day that I do have a thick shell. I've needed it all these years with you.

GEORGE

My friends were right. Our backgrounds *are* too different.

GRACE

That hurts, George, that really hurts. Forgive me, but *I* could say the same thing if I wanted to, you know. I think as much of my heritage as you do of yours. But I wouldn't say that, George. Regardless of how strongly I feel it sometimes, I wouldn't *say* that. I'm not that kind of woman. I'm not mean. *I* wouldn't want to hurt *your* feelings. (*He is silent, hangs his head.*) I know now I was too young to settle down. I didn't have the slightest idea what marriage was all about. But I've let larger values take the place of my immature fantasies. I've risen above all the unpleasant things that have happened. And believe me, there've been a lot. I know all about the other women in your life, George. But I've just shut my eyes and pulled my head in. I've stood humiliation after humiliation, George, because I've always hoped you'd grow up. It hasn't been easy for me, George, but God has helped me through it all. (*He hangs his head lower.*) It was just as big a step for me to take as it was for you. My friends warned me, but I was blinded by love, and I believed you when you said you loved me, and that it didn't matter how different our backgrounds were, that our love would overcome all obstacles.

GEORGE

(*sullenly*) Some things you just can't overcome.

GRACE

You were always the first one to jump up and shout "We shall overcome."

GEORGE

I don't anymore.

GRACE

You're too worked up and tense. Just relax.

GEORGE

How can I, when I know the same horrible thing will happen again . . the next time.

GRACE

All right, George, if we must discuss it, then I have only one thing to say.

13

It is *your* fault. You know it is. You don't concentrate. You're too easily distracted.

GEORGE

I go crazy waiting for you to get started.

GRACE

Pacing, George, pacing is the secret. I just hit a comfortable stride and relax, that's all.

GEORGE

Crawling through life, like you do, isn't enough for me. There's got to be more to life than just the same old routine every day. I need excitement, speed, things happening fast. I'm an action man!

GRACE

We're not teenagers.

GEORGE

What the hell does age have to do with it? I'm just as good as I ever was.

GRACE

Life's reward is in achievement, dear, not spasmodic bursts of speed. And achievement is only gained by planning, by steady pacing. The inconsistent gallop you go at doesn't pay off. You know it doesn't. It's from one extreme to the other with you. That's the same way you are with the children. For five minutes you're the Father of the Year, and then for the next month they never see you. (*He is sulking.*) I'll never, if I live to be one hundred and fifty, forget last Christmas.

GEORGE

What about last Christmas?

GRACE

I can't believe my ears, George. You've got to be kidding.

GEORGE

(*raising his voice*) What about last Christmas?

GRACE

I'm sure if I took a two-day trip without you you'd walk right past me when I got home and never remember who I was.

GEORGE

(*shouting*) What about last Christmas?

GRACE

You really should see Dr. Schlange about this, dear. Your memory is going fast.

GEORGE

(*screaming*) Christmas! Christmas! Christmas!

GRACE

(*made nervous by his screaming*) What about Christmas?

GEORGE

What do you mean — What about Christmas? Jesus Christ, woman, you were making a federal case out of something I can't remember from six months ago and now you can't remember what we were talking about ten seconds ago!

GRACE

It just slipped my mind for the moment.

GEORGE

Now who should see Schlange, huh? Now who?

GRACE

Control yourself, George. Last Christmas Eve, after the children were tucked in their little beds, I left you in the living room to put up the tree and I went upstairs to finish wrapping their Santa Claus. After a while you came up and we went to bed. It never once occurred to me to ask you if you had finished the tree. The next morning I woke up just seconds before the children, just in time to dash downstairs and put the gifts under the tree, only to discover, to my absolute horror — and if I live to be one hundred and fifty I'll never, never, never forget the sinking feeling I had at that moment — to discover, as I said, to my absolute horror, that you hadn't trimmed the tree! Not one light, not one ball, not one icicle. I'll never forget that moment, with the children already on the stairs. And all you could tell me was that you were watching a Disney Special.

GEORGE

(*defensively*) It all worked out okay. The kids had a good time helping decorate the tree. We made it a family project.

GRACE

George, that's not the point, and you know it. It's the same old basic problem with you. You let your mind wander, right in the home stretch. You've got to learn to concentrate. That's all it takes, concentration. Really dear, that's all.

GEORGE

(*very submissively*) You're right. I admit it. I always forget what I'm doing.

GRACE

Well I'll never understand how that happens. When I'm that close I'm about to explode. A woman couldn't possibly get distracted *then*.

GEORGE

Well that's the way I am. It's pointless for us to go on.

GRACE

George, we owe it to ourselves, to the children, to the whole world, to try it once more. (*He is silent.*) Please George . . just once more?

GEORGE

Only if you'll promise me one thing.

GRACE

Anything, George. I'll do anything humanly possible to save our marriage. You know that.

GEORGE

Promise you'll hold back if it starts happening again.

GRACE

I'll try, George, God knows I'll try. But the moment I hear them cheering . . well, something happens and I *can't* hold back.

GEORGE

Maybe if you couldn't hear them . .

GRACE

What do you mean?

GEORGE

Here. Put these carrots in your ears. (*He reaches down into the egg and hands her two carrots.*)

GRACE

That's a marvelous idea. You're a genius, George. Haven't I always said you were a genius?

GEORGE

(*very excited*) Hurry up, put them in.

GRACE

All right. (*She puts a carrot in each ear, smiles at him.*)

GEORGE

Can you hear me? (*She continues to smile.*) (*a little louder*) Can you hear me? (*She just smiles.*) (*shouting*) Can you hear me? (*When she still does not hear he shakes her.*)

GRACE

(*removing carrots*) I'm sorry, dear. I couldn't hear you. What did you say?

GEORGE

I was just testing to see if you could hear me.

GRACE

I couldn't hear a thing. I could see your lips moving, but I couldn't hear a thing.

GEORGE

(*very excited*) Shall we try it now?

GRACE

(*very coy*) Whenever you're ready.

GEORGE

You know I'm always ready.

GRACE

(*seductively*) So am I.

GEORGE

Let's go, baby. (*He puts his hands on the sides of the egg, preparing to stand, as one does in getting out of a bathtub, but she raises her hand to stop him.*)

GRACE

Wait.

GEORGE

What's the matter?

GRACE

I think we ought to ask God's blessing.

GEORGE

Why? What can that silly old bitch do for us?

GRACE

George! She'll hear you.

GEORGE

So what happens then? "Off with his head, off with his head!" (*She begins to cry.*) Oh, all right, if it will make you happy.

GRACE

(*instantly recovering*) Now fold your hands and don't do anything to irritate her this time . . please. (*He reluctantly folds his hands in the traditional prayer attitude; she looks up at the tree and gives a loud whistle through two fingers, then quickly folds her hands too; the stained-glass window lights up as trumpets blast a short chord, ending off-key; the window in the tree flies open and God appears; he is a short, fat, stand-up comic, with a five o'clock shadow, chewing a black cigar, and dressed as the Queen of Hearts, with overly large red lips and cheeks; when the window opens he is caught with a hand mirror and lipstick; he is very impatient, hostile, extremely bored.*)

GOD

Oh, you two again. Don't you know how busy I am? What do you want?

GRACE

Your Majesty, we want to try it once more.

17

GOD

It's a wonder to me you've got the strength left.

GRACE

We want your blessing, Your Majesty.

GOD

(*points a jeweled finger at George*) Speedy Gonzalez too? Does he want my blessing? (*George is not paying attention; she nudges him.*)

GEORGE

Oh. Yes, Your *Divine* Majesty.

GOD

(*furious*) Get smart with me and I'll send you ticks, you heterosexual little freak! (*George shrinks lower into the egg, raising his hands in a prayer attitude to defend himself against God. God snorts, then reaches inside the window, gets a fancy cut-glass atomizer with a bulb at the end of a long rubber tube, and gives one quick squirt over the egg.*) There.

GRACE

Oh thank you, thank you, Your Majesty.

GOD

All right, all right. Let's go. I'm busy, busy, busy. Let's go. (*George hops out of the egg. From his waist down he is a white rabbit. He goes to the front side of the egg and lets down a concealed ramp, then assists Grace out. She is a pink and blue turtle. She places the carrots in her ears. They then get into a starting position under the tree, facing offstage. Grace nods to God that they are ready.*)

GOD

Finally. So on your mark, get set, ready . . (*God fires a tiny pistol which makes a loud bang; the window immediately closes and the light goes off. George begins to quickly hop off right. Grace rises with difficulty to bent legs, toddles after him. When he sees how far behind she is, he turns, laughs, and begins to run a circle around her, then comes to down left and does a cartwheel, kicks up his heels, and dances to the organ music. He does not notice that the carrots fall out of her ears as she is exiting. Suddenly there is wild cheering and shouting offstage when she has exited. A pin spot falls on George, as the general lighting fades. Black lights come up on the flowers, and we see them turn in the direction of the cheering. George realizes what has happened, throws himself on the floor, and is pounding it with his fists and kicking as the lights fade.*)

CURTAIN

Grace and George and God by Alexander Hierholzer opened on April 18, 1970, at Birmingham-Southern College. It was directed by Arnold Powell and designed by John Kitchens.

Cast of Characters

GRACE	Susan Brown
GEORGE	Ed Peed
GOD	Steve Johnson

DAVID BALL

Assassin!

A FABLIAU IN TWO ACTS
Drawn from a Film by Roderick Bradley

for **R and G**

Cast of Characters

PHILLIP	GENTLEMAN
WOUNDED SOLDIER	EDGAR
ARMY OFFICER	AGENT ONE
DOPE SELLER	AGENT TWO
CUSTOMS OFFICER	BARTENDER
PREACHER	GO-GO DANCER
BEGGAR	GUNMAN
FRANZ	PETERSON
MELISSA	COP ONE
PHONE LADY	COP TWO
OLD MAN	FIGURE ONE
GYPSY	FIGURE TWO
NATASHA	STREETSINGER
JASON	SECOND INSPECTOR
GLOUCESTER	

Also PEOPLE IN CUSTOMS OFFICE, SALVATION ARMY BAND MEMBERS, NEW YORK PASSERSBY, KING'S ATTENDANTS, and BAR PATRONS (with actors doubling up, the play can be done with sixteen people)

The Setting

The stage for the entire play has a single setting of abstract design using shapes in space such as thin, irregular pillars; portals cut into the side and back walls; etc. Shapes rising from the stage floor are referred to as "pillars" in the script, although they may be designed in other ways. Attached to one of the pillars is a sign which says "MEN" on one side and "PHONE" on the other. Only one side is visible at a time; the sign may be flipped easily from one side to the other. It may also be moved out of sight.

ASSASSIN!

ACT ONE

The sound effects for the beginning of the play may start very quietly several minutes before curtain time, continue through Phillip's first lines, and then come up to normal level. We do not see Phillip during the first lines; instead we hear his amplified, slightly hollow voice.

PHILLIP

> And what is this, but vacant fantasy?
> And what is this, a state which seems
> A changing act that failing gleams
> With phantom joy, delusive rest?
> The life which is a dream at best
> Knows dreams themselves are only dreams.

(The sounds of a distant battle. Occasional distant bombs dropping cause a wave of dull, throbbing light to wash over the entire stage. After a few moments, we suddenly hear, very close, a machine gun firing. At the second or third spurt of machine-gun fire, Phillip enters, lit by a dim follow-spot light. Phillip is a soldier; he carries a machine gun and, on his back, a knapsack. He is running from the gunner offstage and is obviously terribly frightened. The spurts of gunfire chase him from point to point along the stage; he attempts to find cover behind pillars. Shortly he speaks.) Where is everybody? Where the hell is everybody? *(Continuation of fleeing from machine-gun fire. Phillip's reactions become more and more panicked. As he reacts to the gunfire more and more violently, the machine gunner*

moves slowly away; the gunfire eventually fades into the sounds of the distant battle.) I'm not here, damn you. I'm not here! (*The stage lights come up — perhaps during one of the bomb flashes — to a fairly low level, but enough to allow us to see clearly without the follow-spot. Phillip is crying; lost, desolate, out of his mind. He huddles limply at one edge of the stage. At the opposite end of the stage appears a badly wounded soldier. He staggers a few steps toward Phillip, then falls to his knees. He is unarmed.*)

WOUNDED SOLDIER

Phillip! (*Phillip suddenly tenses; without pointing his gun any particular way, he squeezes the trigger. He swings the gun around with no awareness of what he is doing; he swings it upstage, away from the audience, in a wide arc toward the wounded soldier. Phillip stumbles to his feet as the shooting passes the wounded soldier; the wounded soldier falls dead; Phillip stops shooting; there is silence but for Phillip's breathing — panting. Phillip throws away his gun; goes to the dead soldier and leans over him. Phillip is confused. He backs away in great fright, very slowly, toward his initial position. The lights fade except for a single shaft on Phillip. Phillip breaks the scene abruptly by turning toward the audience as if he'd been aware of it all along. During the following speech, Phillip changes his uniform jacket, shirt, and helmet for a shirt and sports jacket which he carries in the knapsack. He stuffs the uniform into the knapsack and throws it offstage.*)

PHILLIP

All right, let me give it to you straight. If you want to know. My name is deKoch; Phillip deKoch; I used to be a soldier. Until one day I was the only one left; I decided to retire; I went out undefeated. I used to be an actor, too, just before I was a soldier. I'm not sure which was worse; I couldn't understand either one.

And just so you don't misunderstand anything: deKoch isn't my real name. I mean, it's my real name, but I picked it myself. My parents are anonymous; I was an anonymous donation to the Church's foundling collection. I was adopted once when I was eight — I was returned two weeks later. I forgot to flush the toilet or something. But anyway, I had to give myself a name; my parents avoided even that.

Not that I blame them; I don't have any grudge against my old man; he was a coward, obviously. That's why I stopped being a hero. It's in my blood to run away. Heredity yanking me from my environment; I ran away — from that. (*Phillip indicates the dead soldier, who rises, glares at*

ASSASSIN!

Phillip, picks up the machine gun Phillip dropped dropped near him, and leaves.)

WOUNDED SOLDIER

(*as he goes*) Son of a bitch! (*exits*)

PHILLIP

But I can adapt — I can adapt to anything. Hell, there I was, fresh off the wars; walked for three weeks — in a straight line, like the good sisters taught me. My straight line bisected this little town near the border. (*Lights up across the stage: an army officer stands with his back to Phillip. Behind the officer, on the ground, is a stick of wood.*) Used my ingenuity; adaptability. (*Phillip approaches the officer from behind and batters him over the head with the stick; the officer falls. Phillip takes the officer's wallet and returns to his initial position.*) Three hundred bucks — and some baby pictures. I threw them away. Musta' been payday for the guy — standing there with three hundred bucks in his pocket, pictures of his kids — you know, the kind the poor guy hasn't seen since before they were born? — probably waiting for a whore.

ARMY OFFICER

(*rises, glares at Phillip, and leaves*) Son of a bitch! (*exits*)

PHILLIP

Anyway, three hundred bucks, which my adaptability easily converts into greater assets. I make some contacts — (*Phillip disappears into an upstage portal; as he does, we hear Eastern music fading in; also, across the stage, lights come up on an Eastern dope seller; he wears robes, etc., and sits — squats — behind a gigantic water pipe producing great amounts of smoke. From behind him comes Phillip, who leans over him.*) Hashish! Three hundred dollars!

DOPE SELLER

No me; no hash me. (*Phillip grabs the dope seller by the collar, drags him up, looks into his face.*)

PHILLIP

Come on, I see it. Right there, I see it. Three hundred dollars' worth quick. Hashish, quick!

DOPE SELLER

Night, you come back night.

PHILLIP

Now! Or I'll — (*Phillip has his hands around the dope seller's throat and begins to squeeze.*)

DOPE SELLER

Yes, good, now. (*Phillip releases him.*) American, you?

PHILLIP

Yeah; CIA; collecting samples; hurry up.

DOPE SELLER

(*handing Phillip a packet*) Three hundred. (*Phillip gives the dope seller some money. The dope seller runs off in fear and anger. As he leaves, he yells, over his shoulder, in Hindi*) Son of a bitch! (*And the Eastern music fades away.*)

PHILLIP

(*tossing the packet in his hand*) My personal little GI bill. Three hundred here — thousands back home. Only I had to trade off half — eventually — for the right papers and a ticket. (*Phillip moves upstage; at the end of the next line he disappears through a portal.*) But the trip was good; changed ships once; ended up on the good old U.S.S. *Constitution* — every inch a ship and then some. (*Suddenly the entire stage is lit; we are at customs, U.S.A. A group of people, Phillip in the lead, pour out of an upstage portal and line up at the customs counter. During the beginning of this scene we hear, at low volume, the sound of a rather terrible amateur band playing the "Star-Spangled Banner." This sound does not fade; instead, at some point about two-thirds of the way through the scene, the band sort of dies, instrument by instrument. Phillip steps up to the customs counter and regards the inspecting officer.*) Home sweet home.

CUSTOMS OFFICER

Name?

PHILLIP

DeKoch; Phillip deKoch.

CUSTOMS OFFICER

Anything to declare?

PHILLIP

Not a thing.

CUSTOMS OFFICER

Open your suitcase, please, and empty everything in your pockets onto the counter.

PHILLIP

Yes, sir. (*He complies.*)

CUSTOMS OFFICER

How long were you out of the country?

PHILLIP

Three months.

CUSTOMS OFFICER

Business? (*i.e., "What was your business?"*)

PHILLIP

Pleasure.

CUSTOMS OFFICER

Is this all your baggage?

PHILLIP

I travel light.

CUSTOMS OFFICER

(*taking a stuffed doll from the suitcase*) What's this?

PHILLIP

A doll. Stuffed. From Paris.

CUSTOMS OFFICER

I'm afraid I'm going to have to cut it open.

PHILLIP

Cut it open? That's a present for someone.

CUSTOMS OFFICER

Sorry. I'll just cut it along the seam here. It'll be easy enough to sew up.

PHILLIP

I don't sew. (*The customs officer cuts it open.*) What if it's full of intestines?

CUSTOMS OFFICER

We look for everything.

PHILLIP

Do you pay me damages if there's nothing in it?

CUSTOMS OFFICER

(*prodding through the doll's stuffing*) If you'd care to register a reclamation of damages form with us, I'd be glad —

PHILLIP

Skip it.

CUSTOMS OFFICER

Well, I guess you're clean.

PHILLIP

Thanks.

CUSTOMS OFFICER

Keep this health card. If you become sick within the next two years, show it to your doctor.

PHILLIP

Yeah.

CUSTOMS OFFICER

All right; that's all; move along, please. (*Phillip gathers his things and moves downstage. The next woman in line has three or four large suitcases and a poodle. Lights down on the customs area.*)

PHILLIP

(*reading the health card*) "This person has been potentially exposed to rabies, cowpox, diphtheria, smallpox, syphilis, and various uncommon parasitic agents. In case of disease, physical or otherwise, notify the Non-Alien Immigration Bureau." Humph. Home sweet home. (*Phillip opens his suitcase; from his jacket he takes several small packets wrapped exactly like the larger packet of hashish and places them into the suitcase.*) Uncommon parasitic agents. (*Abruptly, we hear the sounds of a Salvation Army band playing "Just a Closer Walk with Thee" — or the equivalent. Lights up on the band and the preacher. The preacher is gaunt and speaks from behind a pulpit on large wheels.*)

PREACHER

(*pointing to Phillip*) You!

PHILLIP

(*statement*) Me.

PREACHER

Yes, you, brother. Divine fate has chosen you for today's lesson in spiritual wit, healing and wisdom.

PHILLIP

(*statement*) Me.

PREACHER

Yes, brother.

PHILLIP

Bit of a coincidence, don't you think?

PREACHER

Coincidence?

PHILLIP

Well, there's no reason or anything why you happened to pick me, is there?

PREACHER

Yes, there is a reason — but it remains concealed in the divine cosmos.

PHILLIP

Oh.

PREACHER

Brother! You are oppressed in your heart! Come unto us; come unto Jesus; be at peace.

PHILLIP

I'm at peace already, thanks.

PREACHER

Quiet! You are at peace — but only in your mind! What about your soul, brother?

PHILLIP

Yeah, well . .

PREACHER

The soul of man moves in dark ways, brother. It is never at peace without Jesus. (*motions Phillip to draw nearer*) Come up a little closer, brother. Step right up here; let me get a look at you. (*Phillip moves slightly closer.*) Ah! Returned from the wars, I see.

PHILLIP

What makes you say that?

PREACHER

Ah! What makes anyone say anything?

PHILLIP

Well, you're wrong. I'm not from any wars.

PREACHER

You can't playact with me, brother. Not with me; not with Jesus, either. We know — there are no secrets! Not on the great stage of life.

PHILLIP

Yeah.

PREACHER

Life is just that, brother. A stage, a play, we are simply players moving about, to and fro, acting out our various roles.

PHILLIP

How did that seep into religion?

PREACHER

Jesus does not seep, my brother. He is the great director of all things; we are his charges; his actors; we must follow that great script inscribed in the heavenly skies! Jesus, my brother.

MEMBER OF THE BAND

Amen to that, brother!

PREACHER

Thank you, brother. (*to Phillip*) Do you know your part, brother?

PHILLIP

Not particularly.

PREACHER

You must discover your part. We all have our roles; we all have our many roles; the destiny of God awaits the rising of the curtain.

PHILLIP

Aren't you sort of milking that dry?

PREACHER

Let not worldly things drag you into the ashes of perdition. Eternal perdition.

PHILLIP

Yeah, look; what do you want?

PREACHER

I want your soul, brother.

PHILLIP

What for?

PREACHER

It needs saving!

PHILLIP

Not now. (*Phillip starts to leave; he is quickly surrounded by the members of the band who coerce him back toward the preacher.*) Now come on! Let go of me.

PREACHER

Sit! (*Phillip is seated by the band members.*) Hallelujah, brother!

PHILLIP

You mind if I smoke?

PREACHER

Let each man sin as he may; he may be saved nevertheless.

PHILLIP

Amen to that, brother.

PREACHER

God (*pause*) commands you (*pause*)to (*pause*) take his part. (*pause*) *You* have a role (*pause*) in the great, eternal cosmos.

PHILLIP

Yeah.

PREACHER

You must find that part! Perhaps you are amongst the blessèd; the chosen of the Lord: YOU MAY HAVE MANY AND MANY PARTS TO PLAY, brother; parts vacated by our pagan neighbors. (*pause*)

PHILLIP

Is that all? Can I go now?

PREACHER

Yea, go from me into everlasting damnation — or go from me and seek what I have bid ye seek. Farewell, brother. (*Phillip rises, comes down-*

stage; lights fade on the preacher and his band as we hear the preacher's last words.) Seek and ye shall find, brother!

PHILLIP

(*alone, and after a pause*) Yeah, well, good old New York. If it's not one thing it's another. (*Across the stage appears a beggar who approaches Phillip.*)

BEGGAR

Hey, buddy . .

PHILLIP

Look, do you mind if I just sit down a second? I'm recovering from something.

BEGGAR

Sure, buddy, sure. (*For a moment the two wait as Phillip recovers.*)

PHILLIP

All right, what do you want, a cigarette?

BEGGAR

No, not any cigarette. Doctor, he told me: no smoking; no cigarette. All I need's a little change, to get me a cup of soup. Ten cents.

PHILLIP

Sure. (*hands him some change*)

BEGGAR

God bless you, mister. God'll bless you; he'll be good to you; take it from me. But stop that smoking; it's not good. Saw a doctor — right up on Park Avenue; the best; he said to me, Jack, he said — Jack ain't my name, he just called me that — he said, Jack, them butts'll kill you surer'n shootin'. Cut 'em out.

PHILLIP

Yeah.

BEGGAR

I don't drink, neither. Not a drop. Never did.

PHILLIP

Good.

BEGGAR

You know what drinking can do to a man? Rots out your brain right out of your skull. Dissolves it; dissolves your brain. Turns it to nitrogen mush.

PHILLIP

Yeah? That so?

BEGGAR

Yeah, that's so, that's so. It'll kill ya, Jack.

31

PHILLIP
Probably.

BEGGAR
Yes, sir.

PHILLIP
Well, good luck. (*Phillip starts to move away.*)

BEGGAR
(*holding him*) You don't drink, do you?

PHILLIP
No; no, I don't. (*Phillip tries to leave.*)

BEGGAR
It will kill you. It will kill you dead. (*The beggar draws his thumb across Phillip's throat.*)

PHILLIP
Never touch it. See you, now. (*Phillip tries to leave.*)

BEGGAR
(*blocking him; reaches into Phillip's pocket for his cigarettes*) And the same with these here cigarettes!

PHILLIP
(*still trying to leave*) Yeah, well, keep 'em.

BEGGAR
(*pockets the cigarettes; then takes Phillip by the lapels, bringing him close and speaking most confidentially*) And don't — no matter what they tell you — don't ride on no airplanes.

PHILLIP
Huh?

BEGGAR
(*releases Phillip abruptly*) That's all I got to say to you, mister. So long, Jack. (*The beggar disappears into the darkness.*)

PHILLIP
Yeah, well, good old New York. It'll get every piece of change you've got, one bum at a time. Except one; one dime I managed to hold on to; had to make a phone call. (*The "MEN" sign lights up; Phillip flips it over to read "PHONE." He leaves his suitcase on the ground behind him. The business of the phone, dialing, depositing a dime, etc., is all in pantomime. After Phillip dials, we hear a phone ringing. Upstage, a light goes on as the phone stops ringing; we discover Franz holding the receiver in his hand (in pantomime). Franz is Eastern European of some sort; he should have a beard; he speaks with a very slight accent.*)

FRANZ

Hello?

PHILLIP

Franz!

FRANZ

Who is this, please?

PHILLIP

This is Phillip.

FRANZ

Phillip! Where are you?

PHILLIP

Here. New York.

FRANZ

I thought you were —

PHILLIP

I was.

FRANZ

It's good to hear you, Phillip. (*Across the stage appears Melissa, a street urchin. She is barefooted and wears a homemade dress. Phillip's back is to her, with the suitcase between them. She approaches the suitcase, snatches it up, and tears away. At the other end of the stage she crouches with a pillar between her and Phillip; she opens the suitcase and begins to prod through its contents. The phone conversation continues with no break.*)

PHILLIP

Yeah. Listen, where can I get rid of some stuff?

FRANZ

Stuff? What stuff?

PHILLIP

You know what I mean, Franz. Stuff.

FRANZ

What kind of stuff?

PHILLIP

Stuff; I've got a load of stuff to get rid of.

FRANZ

Stuffed what?

PHILLIP

Franz. I have in my possession a fortune in — stuff, dammit.

FRANZ

I do not understand you, Phillip. You go away for a long time. You come back. You call me on the telephone and all you can say is "stuff." Stuff. Stuff.

PHILLIP

Look, Franz, I've got a suitcase of —

FRANZ

I know what you've got, Phillip; you've got stuff. Good. Forget it. Congratulations.

PHILLIP

If you can't help me get rid of it you're going to have to lend me five bucks. I just threw away my last ten on —

FRANZ

I have a better alternative.

PHILLIP

I don't understand.

FRANZ

I do. Come over here. We will discuss.

PHILLIP

What do I do with the, uh . . ?

FRANZ

Stuff? What is the difference? Forget it. Come over here; I think I've got something for you.

PHILLIP

What?

FRANZ

Nothing to discuss on the phone.

PHILLIP

How much?

FRANZ

A lot. You'll be interested.

PHILLIP

How much?

FRANZ

Half a million. Cash. (*Phillip takes the receiver from his ear and stares at it. Abruptly the light on Franz goes out. Phillip hangs up and moves slightly downstage.*)

PHILLIP

Ah yes, life's like that. The wheel of fortune; that's something that's survived this century. One minute you're getting shot at, next minute you're getting offered half a million bucks. That's New York! Things like that'd never happen unless you were in New York. Take it from me. Nothing ever happens unless you're in New York. It's the center of something or other.

Ever been in New York on a sunny day? (*Lights up; we are in New York on a sunny day. Melissa is still rummaging through Phillip's suitcase. New York passersby pass by.*) You can walk all over the city for hours; thousands of people; you never meet anyone you know. Of course, there's exceptions — like after I hung up the phone — where was I? Ah, yes, over here. After I talked to Franz — (*But there is a lady talking on the phone.*) Well, just a second. No rush.

LADY

Yes, Gilbert. No, Gilbert. It's impossible, Gilbert. That's irrelevant, Gilbert. All right, Gilbert. (*pause*) You're out of your mind, Gilbert. Goodbye, Gilbert. (*She hangs up; Phillip starts to the phone, but a man cuts in front of him and flips the sign over to read "MEN." The man disappears behind the pillar.*)

PHILLIP

Not like Paris. Nope. Because in New York, you can — (*Phillip flips the sign back to read "PHONE"; the man reappears from behind the pillar zipping up his fly and scowling at Phillip.*) Just like that. (*Phillip takes the phone; Franz reappears as before; they are in mid-conversation.*)

FRANZ

It's a good job for you, Phillip; with all your training.

PHILLIP

Well, we'll see. I'll be there later today.

FRANZ

All right, Phillip.

PHILLIP

Goodbye, Franz. (*Phillip hangs up; lights out on Franz; Phillip turns around, sees his suitcase is gone.*) Hey, my suitcase! (*Melissa is now tossing Phillip's underwear around. Phillip spots her; she grabs the suitcase and begins to run in and around the stage pillars; Phillip chases. Melissa gains; finally they come face to face — at opposite ends of the stage.*) Melissa! (*Phillip pantomimes a gun in his hand — thumb sticking up, index finger pointing at Melissa. Melissa by now has recognized Phillip; he pretends to shoot her. Melissa clutches her stomach — as if shot — doubles over, and falls to the ground. She writhes. The passersby pay no attention at all. Phillip runs up to Melissa, lifts her up and swings her around in his*

35

arms.) Melissa! (*Melissa breaks away from Phillip and holds a packet of hashish up, with a questioning expression.*) Aaah, that's the treasures of my adventures! (*Melissa sniffs at the packet, looking to Phillip for approval.*) That's right; the stuff dreams are made of. Come on, let's get out of here. Where's the old man? (*Melissa points off. They take the suitcase, both of them holding the handle, and run to the far edge of the stage. Melissa goes off alone with the suitcase; Phillip stops and comes downstage. The passersby are all gone; the lights change.*)

It was Melissa, all right. I had Melissa and nearly had half a million bucks, both from that last dime for the phone call. *You* can't find Melissa in New York — or anyplace else, for that matter. Unless she wants to find you, which I doubt. But she found me. She found me. (*Melissa sticks her head back in, wondering where Phillip has gone to. She joins him during the next line.*) We spent that day running through alleys all over lower Manhattan. She never stops, that one. (*to Melissa*) Do you? (*Melissa shakes her head, "no."*) She gets her energy from the ether. (*to Melissa*) Right? (*Melissa holds her nose — ether smells. Lights up upstage; the set is cast in shadows. At one corner of the upstage area sits a very old man — he might be partially within one of the portals. He plays quietly on a recorder or flute. He is unaware of Melissa and Phillip. Phillip speaks as they wander through the set — but not near the old man.*) What happened to your bus? (*Melissa pantomimes that a huge crane picked up the bus and tossed it away; then, something or other came and crushed the bus into a little cube of metal.*) Oh, they cleared the junkyard, huh? (*Melissa nods "yes."*) This where you live now? (*Melissa nods "yes."*) Not bad. What is it? (*Melissa shrugs. In a burst of joy*) Ah, Melissa! (*The old man hears this and stops playing the flute.*)

OLD MAN

What is it? Who's there? (*Melissa leads Phillip to the old man; she places the old man's hand on Phillip's face; the old man feels.*) Phillip? You? Phillip?

PHILLIP

Phillip me Phillip! (*The old man grasps Phillip's hand.*)

OLD MAN

I didn't think we would meet again. Then there was a mistake.

PHILLIP

Must have been.

OLD MAN

How did you get back?

PHILLIP

Traveling-salesman style.

OLD MAN

And now?

PHILLIP

Who knows? Nothing. Rest. My old brain is troubled.

OLD MAN

There is still a war?

PHILLIP

Nope. It's gone. Went out of business.

OLD MAN

Then there was a mistake.

PHILLIP

Yeah. No, no, there's a war.

OLD MAN

Hmm. (*A kind of grunt. Pause; then the old man plays the flute again. Melissa plays with a battered old rag doll.*)

PHILLIP

(*to Melissa*) I had a present for you. But it didn't make it. (*Melissa, disappointed, shrugs. After a moment, Phillip rises and comes downstage. The flute music continues; the lights on the old man and Melissa fade out.*) There must have been a mistake, all right. Would've upset me, awhile ago. I used to believe in that stuff. Went to fortune-tellers all the time. (*Lights up upstage opposite the old man's previous area; we see a gypsy palm-reader. At the end of the next line, Phillip disappears into an upstage portal some distance from the gypsy.*) I thought maybe they really knew something. So I laid down my five bucks like clockwork. (*exits*)

GYPSY

You may come in, now, Mr. deKoch. (*pause*) Leave the cat alone, please. This is quiet hour. (*Phillip enters.*)

PHILLIP

I was just petting it.

GYPSY

Her. And don't. I've told you that before. You never listen to me, Mr. deKoch.

PHILLIP

You never say anything worth listening to.

GYPSY

Then why do you return?

PHILLIP

Who knows? You tell me.

GYPSY

You wouldn't believe me. Perhaps you're just superstitious.

PHILLIP

Yeah.

GYPSY

Accidental wisdom. What do you wish to know today?

PHILLIP

I don't know. You tell me.

GYPSY

Let me see your hand. (*Phillip extends his hand over the table; the gypsy looks at it.*)

PHILLIP

I think my lifeline got longer.

GYPSY

Where?

PHILLIP

There. (*points*)

GYPSY

That line indicates wealth, not life. Immense wealth, Mr. deKoch.

PHILLIP

When?

GYPSY

I can't say.

PHILLIP

Aaaah, big deal. You can't even say if you're right or not, can you?

GYPSY

Not always.

PHILLIP

What's that line? Is that the lifeline?

GYPSY

No.

PHILLIP

What is it?

GYPSY

It could be a lifeline — if you choose to use it.

PHILLIP

Choose — to use it?

GYPSY

It could be a talent, Mr. deKoch. A — special talent.

PHILLIP

Yeah? Maybe. That's how I'll get my immense wealth.

GYPSY

Perhaps all wisdom is accidental; I don't know. (*Suddenly Phillip jumps; yells.*)

PHILLIP

Ow! God damn it! Get away.

GYPSY

I told you to leave her alone. I tell you that every time.

PHILLIP

Goddamn cat. Ought to kill it.

GYPSY

That wouldn't be wise for you.

PHILLIP

It would save this. (*shows blood on his hand*)

GYPSY

Perhaps that is the only way you will learn not to meddle with the cat. Good day, Mr. deKoch. That is all for today, I think.

PHILLIP

Yeah. (*He gives her money.*) So long.

GYPSY

Thank you, Mr. deKoch. (*Phillip comes downstage; lights out on the gypsy.*)

PHILLIP

There are four hundred and eighty-three palm-readers in Washington, D.C. Four hundred and eighty-three. Think about that for a while. Some other time. Anyway, I still have to see Franz. But first; yes, first; there are some arrangements to be made — there is, after all, something I need at the moment more than money — (*Lights up; we are in a theatre dressing and makeup room. With her back to the audience, peering into a makeup mirror, is Natasha, an actress. Phillip comes up behind her and places his hands over her eyes.*)

NATASHA

Jesus Christ, cut the crap, will you?

PHILLIP

Oh, Natasha, *ma belle amour, ma toujours* . .

NATASHA

Lay off! What the hell do you think you're doing? (*She breaks away; turns around.*) Phillip!

PHILLIP

Yeah.

NATASHA

What are you doing here?

PHILLIP

I came to see my little kitten.

NATASHA

I thought you were —

PHILLIP

I was.

NATASHA

— in for two years.

PHILLIP

I haven't been for ten weeks. (*indicates her costume*) Lady Macbeth?

NATASHA

Ophelia.

PHILLIP

Let's get us to a nunnery.

NATASHA

Good, my lord.

PHILLIP

Yeah. I'll see you later — at your place?

NATASHA

You'll need a key.

PHILLIP

It's not under the mat? What if I'd come back? In the middle of the night?

NATASHA

(*handing him a key*) It would have been a bit — awkward.

PHILLIP

Is Bobo still around? I'll kill the son of a bitch.

NATASHA

Phillip! Jealous?

PHILLIP

No. Worried about my health. They show you all kinds of scary movies in the army.

NATASHA

I'll bet.

40

PHILLIP
Yeah, that's why I left.

NATASHA
And came running back to good old Natasha.

PHILLIP
Sure. I missed you — with every foxhole I dug. (*Jason's voice from offstage*: "Places, Act Three.")

NATASHA
See you later.

PHILLIP
Ophelia's not in Act Three —

NATASHA
Is too. (*Phillip grabs Natasha, kisses her. She breaks away.*) Cut it out. You'll mess my makeup. (*Phillip puts his thumb into a makeup jar and spreads a streak of bright orange makeup across Natasha's face.*) You bastard! (*Jason's voice from offstage:* "Places, Act Three.")

PHILLIP
You look charming, my dear.

NATASHA
(*wiping off the orange streak*) Get out of here, will you?

PHILLIP
(*sitting in her chair*) Yeah. (*Natasha leaves; on her way out she bumps into Jason entering.*)

NATASHA
Look where the hell you're going.

JASON
What's the matter with you? (*sees Phillip*) Phillip! What are you doing here?

PHILLIP
Procuring.

JASON
I thought you were — (*pause*)

PHILLIP
Fighting a war?

JASON
Yes. Fighting a war.

PHILLIP
I was. I left.

JASON
Nothing serious, I hope.

41

PHILLIP

No, no — a small disagreement with a comrade.

JASON

Well, anyway, I'm glad to see you back.

PHILLIP

Yeah.

JASON

You want a job?

PHILLIP

Doing what?

JASON

Acting. What else can you do?

PHILLIP

Yeah. No, no, I don't need a job, Jason.

JASON

It's not every day an actor walks into a job like this, you know.

PHILLIP

Like what?

JASON

Hundred a week.

PHILLIP

Yeah?

JASON

That's a lot. Things aren't so good right now.

PHILLIP

I'll think about it.

JASON

You'll go into rehearsal next week.

PHILLIP

Even if I don't take the job?

JASON

(*enticing Phillip*) Othello, Lear, Hamlet, Willy Loman . .

PHILLIP

I don't like to be typecast. Listen, I'll talk to you. I've gotta go.

JASON

Sure.

PHILLIP

Oh, Jason, do me one favor, will you? If anyone asks — I'm not around, as far as you know.

JASON

Sounds cryptic.

PHILLIP

(*leaving, as the lights fade on the area, and coming downstage*) Oh, it is, it is. (*Lights out on dressing room; Phillip is now all the way downstage.*) Cryptic. (*muses over the word*) Cryptic. Everything is cryptic. (*pause*) Nothing's cryptic. Everything's irrelevant. No, that's not quite right. Inconceivable; that's it. Inconceivable; like half a million dollars sitting there waiting. All I have to do for it — (*pause; lights up on Franz's apartment*) is see Franz. (*Phillip walks into the apartment area; Franz hands him a glass of wine; the scene picks up in the middle.*)

FRANZ

And that's all there is to it.

PHILLIP

Half a million bucks. Just like that. What if I get killed?

FRANZ

If you're successful, it'll go to your next of kin.

PHILLIP

Great.

FRANZ

Or someone like that.

PHILLIP

Great.

FRANZ

Phillip, the job needs doing. They've closed the embassy in Washington; it's that bad. My country is nearly in ruin. I had to bring my family here to hide them.

PHILLIP

Mmm. Look, you say, "That's all there is to it." Just casually go shoot the most powerful man in Europe. How?

FRANZ

It's all arranged. You'll be sent to Solond as a neutral correspondent.

PHILLIP

Hiding a high-powered rifle in my pocket.

FRANZ

No rifles.

PHILLIP

I hate pistols.

FRANZ

No guns.

43

PHILLIP

I poison him? Come on.

FRANZ

No poison. It's got to be fast and foolproof.

PHILLIP

I could scare him to death.

FRANZ

Not Frankler.

PHILLIP

All right, how?

FRANZ

Piano wire.

PHILLIP

(*statement*) Piano wire.

FRANZ

You will gain his confidence by your amiable views toward his policies; you will be able to get him alone. Write a few flattering stories about him; let him approve them; he'll love you.

PHILLIP

I get him alone with a piano wire. Great plan. Then what? We play jump-rope until he has a heart attack?

FRANZ

(*pantomiming on Phillip*) You — decapitate him — with the piano wire. That way.

PHILLIP

Goodbye, Franz. Regards to your family.

FRANZ

Phillip. It's the only way. You'll never get a gun within a hundred miles of Frankler.

PHILLIP

How does one conceal piano wire?

FRANZ

In your underwear.

PHILLIP

Are you serious? I thought you were serious. Hell, Franz, I thought you were serious.

FRANZ

In your underwear.

PHILLIP

Sure, there we are, in the middle of a private little tête-à-tête; I whip down my pants and let him have it with the piano wire.

FRANZ

Something like that.

PHILLIP

I quit. So long.

FRANZ

(*producing an envelope*) There is two hundred thousand dollars in small bills in this envelope. Take it. You'll get the remainder afterwards.

PHILLIP

Keep it. You're crazy. (*opens the envelope; looks at the money*) Who's financing this?

FRANZ

There are — patriots.

PHILLIP

I've been through that. (*handles the money, then gives it back to Franz*) Let me think about it.

FRANZ

You have two days. That's all.

PHILLIP

I'll see you. (*lights down on Franz and the apartment as Phillip comes downstage*) Piano wire. Ingenious. (*reaches into his pants*) Just reach into my pants; produce a roll of piano wire. What if he asks me what I'm doing? "Oh, uh, nothing, sir; just an odd American custom; I'm adjusting my piano wire." (*pause*) I wonder if piano wire gets tangled.

Half a million bucks. Well. On the other hand, though, there are certain things even a retired hero is afraid of. I can't take half a million bucks just because it's there — not without talking to my spiritual adviser. (*Lights up on Melissa and the old man. The old man is listening to Phillip talk as Phillip walks into the area.*) . . and then the friendly agents who smuggled me into the country will smuggle me out. And that's all there is to it.

OLD MAN

And what will you do then?

PHILLIP

I will change my name, grow a long white beard, stain my teeth yellow — or perhaps green — and live happily ever after as a humble fisherman in a small whitewashed village on the Mediterranean.

OLD MAN

That sounds good. I hope you will be successful.

PHILLIP
Don't you know?

OLD MAN
No, I don't.

PHILLIP
Why not?

OLD MAN
I don't know. Things aren't the same any more. Everything is hard to see, hard to understand. Remember, I said that you would not come back from the wars.

PHILLIP
That's right. Well, I cheated a little.

OLD MAN
And you may cheat again. Or be cheated.

PHILLIP
Don't you see anything? Anything at all?

OLD MAN
No. Have you seen the gypsy?

PHILLIP
Aaah, the gypsy. She takes my five bucks and tells me I'm going to lose five bucks.

OLD MAN
Yes, well, perhaps.

PHILLIP
What am I supposed to do?

OLD MAN
This man, Frankler, is he evil?

PHILLIP
Franz says he is; a dictator or something. I don't know; how should I know if he's evil? I've never even seen him. What's the difference?

OLD MAN
I'm curious about your motives.

PHILLIP
My motives, my motives: half a million bucks. I'll buy you a country cottage by a stream.

OLD MAN
That is a fine motive. I have never been in the country.

PHILLIP
Yeah, well, we'll see. You have some money for a while, anyway. I gave Melissa some stuff to unload; few thousand; keep you here for a few years.

OLD MAN

I'll be here for a few years with or without it. But thank you, Phillip.

PHILLIP

I won't need it. I'll be living it up at the expense of the friendly agents who're smuggling me in. Then the fishing village.

OLD MAN

When do you go?

PHILLIP

Next week? I don't know. I'll be around.

OLD MAN

Good. Once you go, you will not come back.

PHILLIP

Then you do know something.

OLD MAN

Only that there are no fishing villages in this city. (*The old man plays the flute.*)

PHILLIP

(*after a pause*) What if I don't do it? What if I stay here?

OLD MAN

What would you do?

PHILLIP

Get a job. Like before. Acting.

OLD MAN

If I could see, I would come to watch you act.

PHILLIP

No, you wouldn't. I wouldn't let you. I feel like a fool up there. (*Suddenly the stage is lit for a lush production of* King Lear; *we are in IV, vi. Phillip comes into the area; Gloucester hands him a regal cape, crown, wig, etc., which Phillip dons. As he enters the scene, he is calling*) My fool; what ho, my fool; alas, my poor fool —

GLOUCESTER

    Alack, alack the day!

PHILLIP

    When we are born, we cry that we are come
    To this great stage of fools. — This' a good hat —
    It were a delicate stratagem, to shoe
    A troop of horse with felt. I'll put 't in proof;
    And when I have stol'n upon these son-in-laws,
    Then kill, kill, kill, kill, kill, kill!

(*Enter a gentleman with attendants.*)

47

GENTLEMAN

    O, here he is! Lay hand upon him. Sir,
    Your most dear daughter —

PHILLIP

    No rescue? What, a prisoner? I am even
    The natural fool of fortune. Use me well;
    You shall have ransom. Let me have surgeons;
    I am cut to th' brains —

GENTLEMAN

                  You shall have anything.

PHILLIP

    No seconds? All myself?
    Why this would make a man a man of salt,
    To use his eyes for garden water-pots.
    Ay, and laying autumn's dust.

GENTLEMAN

                  Good sir —

PHILLIP

    I will die bravely, like a smug bridegroom. What!
    I will be jovial. Come, come; I am a king,
    My masters, know you that?

GENTLEMAN

    You are a royal one, and we obey you.

PHILLIP

    Then there's life in't. Come an you get it, you
    shall get it by running. Sa, sa, sa, sa.

(*Phillip exits running.*)

GENTLEMAN

    A sight most pitiful in the meanest wretch,
    Past speaking of in a king!

EDGAR

    Hail, gentle sir.

GENTLEMAN

              Sir, speed you; what's your will?

(*Phillip appears where he exited; he is out of costume and simply stands and watches, smoking a cigarette.*)

EDGAR

    Do you hear aught, sir, of a battle toward?

GENTLEMAN

    Most sure and vulgar; everyone hears that
    Who can distinguish sound.

EDGAR

I thank you, sir.

(*The gentleman exits.*)

GLOUCESTER

You ever-gentle gods, take my breath from me;
Let not my worser spirit tempt me again
To die before you please.

EDGAR

Well pray you, father.

GLOUCESTER

Now, good sir, what are you?

EDGAR

A most poor man, made tame to fortune's blows;
Who, by the art of known and feeling sorrows,
Am pregnant to good pity. Give me your hand,
I'll lead you to some biding.

GLOUCESTER

Hearty thanks;
The bounty and the benison of heaven
To boot, and boot!

(*Edgar and Gloucester exit; Phillip goes upstage; the old man and Melissa
come back into view.*)

PHILLIP

Fools! You think they understand that stuff? You think I understand it?
I played Lear one hundred and eight times, in three separate productions.
To splendid reviews. You think I understood it? (*to the old man*) No, even
if you could see, there's nothing to watch when I'm acting; nothing but me,
making a fool out of myself by playing that I'm not any fool. That I'm
looking for another fool. What ho, my poor fool; crap; useless; useless.

OLD MAN

Perhaps less useless than it appears.

PHILLIP

No, just the opposite. It's completely useless; more useless than you'd believe it's possible for anything to be useless. On stage you've got — control
— you can do anything. If you want a man to be twelve feet tall you just
build him scenery and furniture that's half normal size. The audience can't
judge whether the man's tall or the furniture is small.

OLD MAN

How do they know which you intend?

PHILLIP

That's the beauty of it: you tell them; you simply say, "The man is twelve feet tall," and they will believe you. No questions asked; they just sit there and believe. It's better than church; a little sleight of hand and the audience is ready to believe anything.

OLD MAN

That doesn't seem to be so useless. What more could you want?

PHILLIP

Well, it doesn't work, that's the trouble. It works fine in the theatre; try it someplace else and it doesn't work at all.

OLD MAN

Why not?

PHILLIP

I don't know. There's something in a theatre that lets you make up your own — whatever it is. I say I'm King Lear; everyone believes I'm King Lear. They applaud and pay money to watch me. I say I'm King Lear out on the street, and they put me away where I can't do any harm.

OLD MAN

Not because you're King Lear —

PHILLIP

No; because they don't believe I'm King Lear. That's why acting is useless; foolish; it doesn't work when you're out on the street; people have no faith. That's the trouble with the world; people have no faith.

OLD MAN

And do you? If I tell you I'm King Lear, do you believe me?

PHILLIP

I might. You're blind; you might be.

OLD MAN

And if I said I was Melissa?

PHILLIP

No; Melissa's right there.

OLD MAN

Possibly. Melissa, do your dance. Show Phillip your new dance. (*Melissa jumps for joy.*)

PHILLIP

But I'll know; I'll know that it's simply Melissa doing a dance; that you can't be Melissa because she's Melissa.

OLD MAN

But there could be — you know — more than a single Melissa, couldn't there? Besides, Phillip, Melissa has a certain amount of — control. Do your dance, Melissa. (*Melissa takes stage center; during the later part of the dance, the lights fade on Phillip and the old man, so that by the end of the dance, Melissa is alone on stage. Melissa's dance: The story of Father Abraham and son Isaac; Melissa takes the part of Abraham, or, if done clearly enough, she could do both parts. The story line should run from God's command to sacrifice Isaac, through the journey to the mountain, through the word of God releasing Abraham from the sacrifice. Eliminate the sheep. Abraham, leaving Isaac still tied to the altar, is overjoyed at God's mercy and does a dance of joy and thanksgiving. From moment to moment, however, Abraham — Melissa — glances back to where the imaginary body of Isaac is still alive and squirming. Eventually, Isaac becomes too much of a distraction to Abraham's dance of joy and thanksgiving; Abraham takes a sword and plunges it into Isaac. There is another moment of the exhilarated dance of joy and thanksgiving; then Melissa comes downstage and bows. The music for the dance is from the old man's flute. With Melissa's bow, the lights fade, and the curtain falls.)*

ACT TWO

A follow-spot from the upstage wings picks up Melissa doing a few more moments of her dance of joy and thanksgiving. After a time, from upstage come some annoying noises; Melissa glances back to see what is making the noise, but she can see nothing. The noises, as they become more distinct, are the grunts and groans of someone being beaten. Melissa tries to dance on; shortly the old man feels his way into the ring of the follow-spot, and leads Melissa off. For a split second the stage is dark; then the lights come up suddenly on Phillip, tied to a chair, and the two mysterious agents who are beating him. There is blood on Phillip's face. One of the two agents holds a match which he lit exactly as the lights came up. He is lighting a cigarette.

AGENT ONE
Talk!

PHILLIP
About what?

AGENT TWO
(gibberish) I'm getting tired of this. Let's go out for a cup of coffee. *(Note: "gibberish" direction for the agents means that they speak in nonsense syllables. The tone of what they are jabbering, however, should correspond to the given English dialogue.)*

AGENT ONE
(gibberish) In a few minutes.

AGENT TWO

(*to Phillip; no gibberish*) Talk!

PHILLIP

About what?

AGENT ONE

(*gibberish*) All right, let's go get that coffee now. (*The two agents leave. Phillip squirms out of the ropes; stands up; the lights dim upstage as he comes downstage, wiping the blood from his face with a towel which was under the chair.*)

PHILLIP

Up till now, I'd always thought that blood smelled like rosewater, and was kind of thick, and didn't run much. Ah well, we live and learn. See, it's because I was an actor; you can't expect an actor to actually bleed onstage; that's too much. Now, some actors — and lots of actresses, my God, you'd be amazed how many actresses — cry real tears. With some, it's not even a trick; they get themselves worked up and involved and really cry. Not me, though. I never could. I had to learn one of the tricks — you blink your eyes, and stare into a spotlight, and pretty soon you're crying — well, at least there's tears. That's what I did; no one ever knew the difference. I was called an actor of great depth and emotion. Blinking and staring at the spotlights. I can even make myself sneeze if I look at the sun — but of course that doesn't work onstage.

So one way or another actors manage to cry tears. But blood? That's a different story. What we use is this stuff called panchromatic blood. It's made out of glycerine and rosewater; looks real enough from the audience, I guess. And after you've been using it for long enough, you start believing that that must be what real blood is like. In the old days, I'm told, they used ketchup, but ketchup has serious drawbacks. It smells like ketchup; there's not an actor in the world can convince himself — or even the audience — he's really bleeding when he feels like a hamburger. But when you finally convince yourself that this sticky sweet rosewater must be what blood is like, then you're acting; then you've got depth; then you're an actor. Not that it ever does any good. (*He throws the towel into the wings.*) Then all of a sudden you bleed in real life, for some reason or other; you discover that blood is not rosewater. Blood doesn't smell as nice, among other things. It can be quite a shock. That's why acting is useless.

It's like when you get beaten up in a play; you know who it is who's beating you up; you know why they're beating you up; it's all very clear; you just ask the director. But in real life — or whatever it is — it's different. Those guys, for example. I have no idea who they were, what they wanted, why they were beating me up — in other words, all my acting was useless; my blood did not smell like rosewater. In other words, acting does not work. Wisdom for the day: acting does not prepare you to take your place in society. Not like tending a bar, for instance. (*Phillip goes upstage; lights up; we are in a bar. Behind the bar is the bartender; there are a few patrons; on a platform is a go-go dancer dancing to a rock and roll song. Franz is sitting at a table; Phillip joins him.*)

FRANZ

You came after all.

PHILLIP

You know anything about two guys who go around beating people up?

FRANZ

Were you —

PHILLIP

I was. Who were they?

FRANZ

Could be almost anyone. That means we must move quickly. Have you decided?

PHILLIP

No.

FRANZ

Decide. Now.

PHILLIP

Let me get a drink. (*to bartender*) Hey, bartender —

BARTENDER

Self-service, here.

PHILLIP

(*rising, going to the bar*) I want a drink.

BARTENDER

(*sweetly*) Isn't that nice? Anything in particular, or would you like the special of the day?

PHILLIP

Which is?

BARTENDER

Milk and potato juice with cinnamon. And a cookie.

PHILLIP

Yeah, that sounds good. I'll have one of those.

BARTENDER
How old are you?

PHILLIP
What? Old enough.

BARTENDER
You look too old to me. For the special of the day, that is.

PHILLIP
Well, how about a little glass of vodka and tomato juice, then?

BARTENDER
I only have prune juice.

PHILLIP
Fine. Prune juice.

BARTENDER
It's much better with rum.

PHILLIP
Anything. I don't care. Give me a drink, will you?

BARTENDER
How about my invention? The special of the week.

PHILLIP
Whatever you want. I'm in your hands.

BARTENDER
Vodka and tea.

PHILLIP
Tea?

BARTENDER
With vodka.

PHILLIP
Rum and prune juice might be better.

BARTENDER
I never heard of rum and prune juice.

PHILLIP
It's called a Jamaican trot. All the rage in London.

BARTENDER
You'll be happier with tea and vodka.

PHILLIP
I never heard of tea and vodka.

BARTENDER
I just invented it. It's called a tea-totaler.

PHILLIP
Well, now, that sure is clever. Yes, sir. You ought to patent that.

BARTENDER

Well, what'll it be?

PHILLIP

How about a beer?

BARTENDER

What kind?

PHILLIP

How do I know what kind? A glass of beer. Come on, I'm in a hurry.

BARTENDER

All right, grouch. (*grumbles to himself as he gets the beer*) Some guys just hate to pass the time with you — hell with 'em. (*gives Phillip the beer*) Here you are, sociable.

PHILLIP

Thanks. (*pays and rejoins Franz*)

FRANZ

Well?

PHILLIP

Jamaican trot? Or tea-totaler?

FRANZ

What?

PHILLIP

What happens if I say no?

FRANZ

I would have to trust you to keep your mouth shut. Unfortunately, there are some people who might not trust you; I would advise you to say yes.

PHILLIP

Franz, my old friend, you are mixed up with some not very nice people. Is someone threatening me if I say no?

FRANZ

No one is threatening you. But you never know.

PHILLIP

You never do, do you? Well, all right; why not? I'll take your job.

FRANZ

I knew you would, Phillip. I have not known you all these years for nothing. The people of my country will one day publicly revere you.

PHILLIP

Swell.

FRANZ

All right. (*gives Phillip a slip of paper*) Go to this address tomorrow at five o'clock. You will meet two concerned individuals who will give you all the instructions and materials you will need.

PHILLIP

Like piano wire, huh?

FRANZ

Shh. Phillip! This is not a matter to be discussed in public. We shall say no more about it. (*Downstage in the shadows of the corner of the stage appears a man with a revolver which has a long silencer on it. He points the gun at Franz and shoots. Franz flies backwards off his chair; Phillip takes cover behind the table; everyone in the bar is screaming; havoc, etc. The dancer stands on her platform and screams. The screaming continues as the lights go out; several more shots are fired. A rather dim follow-spot picks up Phillip crawling alone to the other edge of downstage. The follow-spot gets brighter as Phillip comes downstage; he finally stands up.*)

PHILLIP

Franz was shot. Dead. They shot him. I felt for him in the dark; his neck was gone. He was dead. (*Cross-fade to the other end of the stage; sitting at his desk is Inspector Peterson. He is a police inspector. A phone rings; Peterson picks it up — in pantomime.*)

PETERSON

Inspector Peterson here. Yes, chief. Yes, I have that file. Right here. Sure. "DeKoch, Phillip. Suspected desertion; Case Number 3584-j." (*pause*) Yes, chief. Right. Natasha Nook; good; I'll get over and see her right now. (*pause*) No, chief, not even a picture. We're working on it. Right. I'll let you know. (*Lights out on the inspector; lights up on Natasha in the theatre dressing room. She is pacing back and forth rehearsing some lines. She acts out her own lines, then punches a tape recorder button. The tape recorder reads the other actor's lines in a flat, mechanical voice.*)

NATASHA

Villain, thou know'st not law of God nor man.
No beast so fierce but knows some touch of pity.

RECORDER

But I know none, and therefore am no beast.

NATASHA

Oh wonderful, when devils tell the truth!

RECORDER

More wonderful, when angels are so angry.
Vouchsafe, divine perfection of a woman,
Of these supposed crimes to give me leave
By circumstance but to acquit myself.

NATASHA

> Vouchsafe, defus'd infection of a man,
> For these known evils but to give me leave
> By circumstance to curse thy cursed self.

RECORDER

> Fairer than tongue can name thee, let me have
> Some patient leisure to excuse myself.

NATASHA

> Fouler than heart can think thee, thou canst make
> No excuse current but to hang thyself.

RECORDER

> Gentle Lady Anne,
> To leave this
> And fall something into a slower method,
> Is not the causer of the timeless deaths
> Of these Plantagenets, Henry and Edward,
> As blameful as the executioner?

NATASHA

> Thou wast the cause, and most accurs'd effect.

RECORDER

> Your beauty was the cause of that effect;
> Your beauty that did haunt me in my sleep —

(*There is a knocking from outside, and we hear the inspector's voice.*)

PETERSON

Miss Nook —

RECORDER

> To undertake the death of all the world
> So I might live one hour in your sweet bosom.

NATASHA

(*turning off the recorder*) Jesus Christ, what is it now?

PETERSON

(*entering*) I'm sorry to disturb you, Miss Nook. (*shows her his badge*) I'm Inspector Peterson.

NATASHA

Isn't that cute?

PETERSON

I'm afraid I have to ask you some questions.

NATASHA

Nothing to be afraid of.

PETERSON

I hope I'm not disturbing you.

NATASHA

Oh, no, no; I was just rehearsing a funeral, that's all. No bother. (*pause*) Well? Ask your questions. Whatever it is, I probably didn't do it yet.

PETERSON

Well, first of all, do you know a Mr. Phillip deKoch?

NATASHA

Do I know a Mr. Phillip deKoch? Why yes; yes, I believe I do.

PETERSON

From where do you know him?

NATASHA

From right here. He used to work here. Actor.

PETERSON

Have you seen him lately?

NATASHA

Umm, no; not to my knowledge.

PETERSON

Not to your knowledge?

NATASHA

No, not to my knowledge.

PETERSON

Does that mean that you may have seen him — *not* to your knowledge?

NATASHA

Why yes; yes, I suppose it does. Perhaps. Mr. deKoch is a master of deception; why he could even be you. (*coming very close to Peterson*) You aren't deKoch, are you? Come on, now; the truth.

PETERSON

No, I assure you I am Inspector Peterson.

NATASHA

Oh come on now; I can see right through you, Phillip. Come and sit down; it's so nice to see you again.

PETERSON

Uh, Miss Nook —

NATASHA

When did you get back? (*draws Peterson to a chair, sits in his lap*) Now tell little Natasha all about how it was.

PETERSON

(*rising; Natasha goes flying*) Now look! I am not Mr. deKoch. Just get that out of your head. I am Inspector Peterson of the twelfth precinct.

NATASHA
Really? That's too bad.

PETERSON
Now, have you or have you not seen Mr. deKoch?

NATASHA
You're not him?

PETERSON
Don't be silly.

NATASHA
Well, then, I guess I'll just have to say no; I have not seen him.

PETERSON
Well. All right.

NATASHA
Is that all?

PETERSON
Yes. No. If you should see him, call this number, please. (*hands her a slip of paper*) Ask for Inspector Peterson.

NATASHA
Peterson; that's your name, isn't it?

PETERSON
Yes.

NATASHA
Hmm. All right.

PETERSON
Thank you, Miss Nook. I'm sorry to disturb you. Good day. (*Peterson exits quickly. Natasha turns the recorder on again.*)

RECORDER
. . live one hour in your sweet bosom.
(*lights begin to fade*)

NATASHA
If I thought that, I tell thee, homicide,
These nails should rend that beauty from my cheeks.
(*Lights down; then up on one corner of the stage: the two agents who beat up Phillip.*)

AGENT ONE
(*gibberish — as is this entire scene*) How do you suppose he got away?

AGENT TWO
He is an American; all Americans can get away.

AGENT ONE
Headquarters will not be happy with us.

59

AGENT TWO
With you, you mean. I am only your assistant.

AGENT ONE
Don't try to blame it all on me.

AGENT TWO
Who should I blame it on? Me?

AGENT ONE
Aaaaah. Do you want a cigarette? (*offers a cigarette*)

AGENT TWO
No thanks. That's one of those menthols, isn't it?

AGENT ONE
Yes; new long Menthol Fresh.

AGENT TWO
Well, I'll try one. Doubt if I'll like it.

AGENT ONE
(*lighting Agent Two's cigarette*) They're as fresh as spring.

AGENT TWO
Say, that's quite a taste.

AGENT ONE
Yes, sir.

AGENT TWO
And mild, too. What did you say they're called?

AGENT ONE
Menthol Fresh.

AGENT TWO
Well. Thanks for the tip. (*Lights fade; back up on the bar. The dancer is standing on her platform, looking horror-stricken at the body of Franz, which Inspector Peterson is inspecting. The room is full of cops; the bartender is also there.*)

PETERSON
How long has he been dead?

ANOTHER COP
A while, now.

PETERSON
Any witnesses?

DANCER
Me! I saw it all!

PETERSON
Come down here, will you?

60

DANCER

Oh no, sir; I couldn't. I don't want to go near it.

PETERSON

Very well. What did you see?

DANCER

Well, the body was sitting there — it wasn't a body then; it was this nice-looking gentleman — with a sneaky-looking fellow who had a gun. Then the fellow shot him.

PETERSON

(*to bartender*) Got a phone? (*The bartender flips out the* "PHONE" *sign.*)

BARTENDER

Right here.

PETERSON

Thanks. (*dials*) Chief? Peterson. I've got a three-eight-five on deKoch; it's his fingerprints. Yes, sir. All right; we've got his description, I'll get out an all-points. (*We hear a siren; lights out on the bar, back up on the two agents; they are smoking and exchanging cigarettes. They hear the siren drawing closer; they look at each other.*)

AGENT ONE

(*gibberish*) What's that?

AGENT TWO

(*no gibberish*) Cops! (*The agents flee across the stage; the siren grows louder; they flee back to where they started from; then exit. The stage is dark; a follow-spot picks up Phillip dashing for cover from pillar to pillar; the siren grows louder; Phillip hides far upstage. The sirens stop; car doors open and slam in the wings. We hear dogs barking and growling. Enter two cops with searchlights.*)

COP ONE

Bring the dogs!

COP'S VOICE

(*from offstage*) They won't get out of the car.

COP TWO

He ain't around here, then. They'd smell him. (*The cops exit; doors open and close again, cars start; the siren starts, fades into the distance. Phillip creeps out.*)

PHILLIP

Smell me! For Christ's sake. Smell me! (*pause*) Well, maybe. It's been a long day. (*Lights on upstage; it's the old man and Melissa in their usual area. They are lit very dimly; Phillip does not turn to them, he stays downstage.*)

61

OLD MAN
Phillip, is that you?

PHILLIP
Yeah, what can you, smell me?

OLD MAN
How are things going?

PHILLIP
Not so good, old man. Franz was just killed.

OLD MAN
Then you are going to take the job?

PHILLIP
I'd already decided to.

OLD MAN
Why?

PHILLIP
It's something that needs doing.

OLD MAN
What did you say?

PHILLIP
It's something that needs doing.

OLD MAN
What are you talking about? What is that supposed to mean?

PHILLIP
Frankler is an evil man. He had Franz killed.

OLD MAN
Then Franz was an evil man; he wanted Frankler killed.

PHILLIP
Yeah, but Franz was my friend.

OLD MAN
Will we see you before you go?

PHILLIP
I don't know. I'm being followed. It might not be safe.

OLD MAN
By who?

PHILLIP
You name it. Cops, Frankler's men, Franz's friends; by now even the army
should be tailing me.

OLD MAN
Try to see us before you go.

PHILLIP

I'll try.

OLD MAN

Phillip —

PHILLIP

Yeah?

OLD MAN

It's not anything that needs doing.

PHILLIP

Yeah, yeah, I know. But I've got to say something.

OLD MAN

It pays a lot of money, doesn't it?

PHILLIP

A good deal; yes.

OLD MAN

Then that's why.

PHILLIP

Probably.

OLD MAN

You will need a lot of luck.

PHILLIP

Yeah.

OLD MAN

Break a leg.

PHILLIP

This isn't exactly a play.

OLD MAN

Perhaps. Try to see us before you go.

PHILLIP

Yeah. (*Lights down on the old man and Melissa. Suddenly Melissa appears near Phillip; she is dancing; the old man's flute plays very quietly. Phillip leans against a pillar and watches, relaxing; he is here talking to himself rather than to the audience; Melissa continues to dance.*) The nice thing about never doing anything is that it's predictable. I envy people who never do anything. They don't have to worry about motivation, for example. You just sit there, all day, day after day. Maybe you stare out a window at a tree. That must be nice. Just — watch the tree grow. You get hungry, you eat an old cracker or something. Pleasant; an aware oblivion. Not like this thing I've gotten into. (*pause; then*) That was another nice thing about acting. You always knew why you were doing something — or at least you pretended you did, which is the same thing. (*Melissa is some distance from Phillip; still dancing. She disappears abruptly as, at the other end of upstage, a light comes up on the gunman who shot Franz.*)

GUNMAN

All right, deKoch. Put your hands over your head. (*Phillip complies; the gunman comes downstage.*) Thought you could avoid me, huh?

PHILLIP

No, not really.

GUNMAN

It'll be easier for both of us if you don't try anything funny.

PHILLIP

I'll bet.

GUNMAN

You want it in the back, or front?

PHILLIP

You mean I get my choice?

GUNMAN

Yeah, why not? I got nothing personal against you. I'm just doing my job.

PHILLIP

Nice guy.

GUNMAN

Don't get mad at me. If it wasn't me, it'd be someone else — who might not give you any choice.

PHILLIP

That's true.

GUNMAN

Now me, for instance; I can't think of nothing worse than getting shot in the back. I got to know what's coming.

PHILLIP

Well, do me a favor, will you? Put the gun real close; it's not so messy that way.

GUNMAN

Oh, one of them, huh? Sure thing. Where?

PHILLIP

(*indicating his backside*) About here?

GUNMAN

No, that won't kill you.

PHILLIP

(*guiding the gunman's hand to Phillip's temple*) How about here?

GUNMAN

Yeah, that's fine. You won't hardly feel a thing. You ready?

PHILLIP

No, just give me a second. I've gotta think my last thoughts. (*Phillip takes a great amount of time with his last thoughts. The gunman looks at his watch.*)

GUNMAN

Hey, come on, I ain't got all day.

PHILLIP

Just a second more, please. (*The gunman looks at his watch again; Phillip ducks and grabs the gun away.*) Well, well. (*The gunman starts to back away.*) Hold it there.

GUNMAN

No sense killing me, buddy. There's others'll get you if I don't.

PHILLIP

I'm not going to kill you. I'm going to hire you.

GUNMAN

Hire me?

PHILLIP

Yeah. I need a bodyguard, that's for sure.

GUNMAN

I come expensive.

PHILLIP

(*indicating the gun*) How much?

GUNMAN

Well, to you, cheap. Five hundred a day.

PHILLIP

Suppose I give you a week in advance right now?

GUNMAN

You got a deal.

PHILLIP

All right. Turn around.

GUNMAN

But I thought you said . .

PHILLIP

I'm not going to shoot you. I want to get the money; it's in my underwear.

GUNMAN

So?

PHILLIP

So I embarrass easily. Please turn around.

65

GUNMAN

All right, but look, no shooting in the back. If you want to shoot, shoot right now. I couldn't stand it in the back.

PHILLIP

Don't worry about it. Pure business; I've got nothing against you personally. Besides, now you're working for me.

GUNMAN

All right. (*turns around*) Get the money. (*Phillip shoots the gunman in the back six times.*)

PHILLIP

It works! (*Phillip moves away from the body; lights fade on the body. Phillip tosses the gun into the darkness at the body.*) It works! It actually works. My God. Well, now for my piano wire. (*Phillip starts upstage as if going into a new scene; then he stops, speaks again.*) I'm starting to get a feeling of accomplishment about all this. Like when you've worked hard all day and you come home at night and you sit in your easy chair and reflect on all the problems you've solved that day, and all the things you've achieved. You feel like it's preordained that you be the great achiever; sitting there; you feel — relaxed and — powerful.

It was the good sisters, that's what. They made me take piano lessons. Every week this little old deaf man came to the orphanage to give me a piano lesson. Taught me the intricacies of piano wire — (*Phillip turns upstage. At each side of the stage, with Phillip in the center and slightly downstage, two figures appear in the shadows. In front of each figure is a small table. The figures speak with an accent like Franz's, but stronger. Figure One is a woman; Figure Two is a man.*)

FIGURE ONE

Until you are safely out of the United States you will carry this gun. (*tosses a revolver onto the table*) It is an old but dependable weapon.

FIGURE TWO

Here is your passport and your papers as correspondent. The work has been well done; you will have no trouble. (*places them on the table*)

FIGURE ONE

You will be perhaps happy to know that the two men who attacked you have been eliminated.

PHILLIP

Overjoyed.

FIGURE TWO

Here is the assassination weapon. (*tosses a coil of piano wire on the table*) It is the finest quality and has been thoroughly tested.

PHILLIP

Swell.

FIGURE ONE

I do not know what your motives are, Mr. deKoch. We know only that Franz was most fond of you and trusted you completely.

FIGURE TWO

Your mission will change the course of history for millions of people, Mr. deKoch. If you are successful, of course.

PHILLIP

Of course.

FIGURE ONE

You will take the eight A.M. flight to Paris; this is your ticket. (*places the ticket on the table*) From there you will be escorted by our agents to Solond.

FIGURE TWO

Here is a list of contacts which you will memorize and destroy before you leave New York. (*places the list on the table*)

FIGURE ONE

You will have no trouble in Solond. There are many who support our cause and stand ready to help you.

FIGURE TWO

It is only fair to tell you that two before you have tried and were not successful. We hope you will have better luck.

PHILLIP

Yeah. Thanks.

FIGURE ONE

You must be careful. There is a saying in our country: "The third time or never."

FIGURE TWO

The importance of this mission cannot be overemphasized. If all goes well, the people of Solond will one day be able to publicly revere you.

PHILLIP

Yeah?

FIGURE ONE

Goodbye, Mr. deKoch. And good luck.

PHILLIP

Thanks. (*The figures exit; Phillip takes the materials from the tables; lights out on the tables as Phillip comes downstage examining the gun.*) "An old but dependable weapon." Hmm. (*Phillip shoots the gun directly into the air; then looks up as if he expects to see something falling out of the sky. He shoots and looks again. Then he shrugs; turns; walks upstage as the lights come up on Natasha's theatre dressing room.)* Hi. Goodbye.

NATASHA

Phillip!

PHILLIP

In the flesh.

NATASHA

(*holding up a newspaper; Phillip ignores it*) How did this happen?

PHILLIP

What?

NATASHA

Murder! Look at this; you're on the front page.

PHILLIP

(*looking at the paper*) What do you know? I'm famous!

NATASHA

You've got to get out of here; you've got to hide. I've been questioned; the police, the army — other people —

PHILLIP

No problem. I leave tomorrow.

NATASHA

Leave! For where? (*knock at the door; she speaks sweetly*) Who is it?

PETERSON

(*from outside*) Inspector Peterson; sorry to disturb you again —

NATASHA

Oh, no bother. Just a moment, please. (*Natasha indicates a direction for Phillip to go hide, offstage.*)

PHILLIP

I can't get out that way —

NATASHA

Just hide there. I'll get rid of him. (*Phillip goes off opposite the side the inspector will enter from. Natasha lets the inspector in.*)

PETERSON

I'm sorry to disturb you again, Miss Nook —

NATASHA

You're not disturbing me. A girl likes a little excitement in her life — inspector.

PETERSON

Mmm. Yes. Well, have you seen Mr. deKoch?

NATASHA

Um, no; no, I'm afraid I haven't . .

PETERSON

It's rather urgent that I find him. He's a suspect in a murder case — and I'm also afraid that his life may be in danger.

NATASHA

Well, if I should see him, I'll be sure to tell him — (*Enter Phillip dressed as King Lear; robes, wig, crown, etc.*)

PHILLIP

What ho! What gentleman waits upon my lady?

PETERSON

(*slightly off center*) I'm looking for a Mr. Phillip deKoch.

PHILLIP

I caught word that he died, last yesterday, or before, and was resurrected on the morrow — though no oracle has mouthed the wherewithal.

PETERSON

You know Mr. deKoch?

PHILLIP

He cannot be known! Or, should it be truer said, I do not know the scoundrel. Though I've been in hearing of him —

PETERSON

May I ask your name, sir?

PHILLIP

Lear! A king, by occupation. But now, my lord, I must beg my leave, my masters, lest I be absent for my exit. What ho, my fool — what ho, my poor fool — Alas, my poor fool! (*Phillip exits, running.*)

PETERSON

(*to Natasha*) Who was that?

NATASHA

Oh, just an actor here. Quite a character.

PETERSON

Sure is. Well, if you run into deKoch, let me know.

NATASHA

Yes sir, inspector. (*Peterson starts to exit; then the bell rings in his mind.*)

PETERSON

Miss Nook —

NATASHA

Yes, inspector?

PETERSON

(*patiently*) That was deKoch, wasn't it?

NATASHA

Who do you mean, inspector?

DAVID BALL

PETERSON

That was him! He was right here and you let him get away.

NATASHA

I didn't know. If that was Phillip, he was disguised as another actor playing King Lear — (*From offstage we hear Phillip's laugh; it is a joyful laugh; very slightly demoniacal.*)

PETERSON

DeKoch! Come back here! (*Peterson exits running with his gun drawn; Natasha is laughing. Lights down on the dressing room, but Natasha's laugh continues. After a pause, Phillip runs across the front of the stage; his robes are swirling; he is ripping off the costume as he goes; exits. Shortly Peterson enters running; sees the "PHONE" light; stops; dials.*) Chief? Peterson. I've found deKoch. He's fleeing — running away. (*pause*) I'll get him, don't worry. (*pause*) No, I don't need any help; I can do this myself. (*hangs up, comes to stage center, calls into the wings*) All right, deKoch, I know you're there. Come out with your hands up. (*Enter the beggar, from Act One.*)

BEGGAR

Hey buddy . .

PETERSON

Not now; I'm busy. (*yells offstage*) DeKoch!!

BEGGAR

Just a dime for a cup of soup, buddy — (*He grasps Peterson's coat.*)

PETERSON

Let go of me; this is official business.

BEGGAR

The guy in the crazy suit, huh? I seen him. He went through there.

PETERSON

(*trying to break away*) Let go, damn you!

BEGGAR

Ten cents, buddy, ten cents. I'll tell you which way he went.

PETERSON

(*giving the beggar some change*) Here; which way?

BEGGAR

(*points off left*) That way; right up through there. (*Peterson exits left, running. The beggar hobbles off right; then, from the right, we hear Phillip's laugh, as before, with a touch more of evil in it. The inspector enters again from the left.*)

PETERSON

That was deKoch! (*Phillip laughs again; the inspector runs off right toward the laugh; he returns again when Phillip's laugh is heard from the left. Peterson carefully searches around the downstage areas; over the apron, etc. Then he exits. Lights and sound up on the bar; the go-go girl is dancing; several men around the bar watch; Peterson enters, looks around, lifts the heads of a few drunks expecting one to be Phillip; goes to the bartender.)*

PETERSON

You see anybody come in here?

BARTENDER

Yeah, yeah, all the time.

PETERSON

Don't be funny; I'm a policeman. I'm looking for deKoch.

BARTENDER

What's that?

PETERSON

Guy about this tall; wearing a beggar's costume.

BARTENDER

No, no, I ain't seen anyone like that. (*The music ends; the dancer bows, the men applaud slightly; she wriggles down from her platform and exits.*)

PETERSON

He might be wearing something else, too.

BARTENDER

Look, cop, I run an honest, peaceful place. I don't know nothing from nothing.

PETERSON

I'll bet. I know your kind. Where is he? (*We hear a girl scream from behind the go-go dancer's platform. Peterson dashes behind the platform; we see him removing his coat; soon he comes out with the go-go dancer who has Peterson's coat wrapped around her. She is huddled into the coat as if she's naked beneath.*) What happened?

DANCER

I don't know. One minute I was dancing; next minute I was lying back there with all my clothes gone. (*dreamily*) I thought I was dreaming. He told me to keep quiet.

PETERSON

He? Who? (*From offstage, Phillip's laugh; it is growing more and more evil. Peterson dashes off. The bartender returns behind the bar; everyone else in the room is watching the inspector, so no one sees the arm which comes up from behind the bar and drags the bartender down. An instant later the bartender reappears behind the bar. Peterson reenters.*)

71

DANCER

Did you find him?

PETERSON

Not yet. But he can't get far. Not dressed like that. (*The dancer wanders toward her platform; she happens to glance behind the bar; she looks at the bartender; then she screams and points at him. The bartender rushes out; Peterson looks behind the bar, exits running after the bartender. The dancer goes behind the bar, bends over.*)

DANCER

(*crying, screaming, etc.*) Max, you all right? Max — speak to me, Max. (*Enter the beggar.*)

BEGGAR

(*looking around*) Eh, what's going on in here? Man comes in off the cold streets for a little cup of soup, he wants peace; peace and quiet. That's the trouble with things nowadays; honest man doesn't have a chance. Screaming and crying everywhere. (*to dancer*) You there; what's going on back there?

DANCER

He's dead; he's dead!

BEGGAR

Dead? Someone dead? What about my soup? I've got to have soup.

DANCER

Help, he's dead.

BARTENDER

(*rising*) I'm not dead. (*He's in his underwear.*) That bastard. Give me that coat, will you?

DANCER

No!

BEGGAR

Here, take mine. And get me a cup of soup. (*The bartender dons the beggar's coat.*)

BARTENDER

Thanks.

BEGGAR

Yeah, sure; give me a cup of soup, will you?

BARTENDER

It's in back; I'll get you some. (*The bartender goes to exit left; Peterson runs in from the right and sees the bartender in the beggar's coat, which he mistakes for Phillip's disguise. Peterson draws his gun and shoots. The bartender turns and stares at the inspector as he dies; the inspector ex-*

pects the bartender to change into Phillip before his eyes. The bartender dies; slight pause; then)

BEGGAR

You shot him.

DANCER

(screaming) Call the police! Call the police!

PETERSON

I am the police. Stay away from that phone. *(spots the beggar)* You! You're —

BEGGAR

Ain't nobody; get away from me with that gun.

PETERSON

Put up your hands. *(Phillip's laugh from offstage right; almost savage. Peterson starts off right; changes his mind, exits left. Seconds later Phillip, dressed as Phillip, runs in from the left and runs off right with Peterson in pursuit; the lights fade out on the bar. Downstage left appears an old black streetsinger with a guitar and begging cup. The old man sits at his feet. The streetsinger is singing in the traditional black streetsinger style; the old man plays along on his flute.)*

STREETSINGER

(singing) Life is just a bowl of cherries . . *(Peterson enters from upstage; stops; draws his gun.)*

PETERSON

You two there! Put up your hands!

OLD MAN

What is it?

STREETSINGER

We ain't got no money, boss. Nothin' at all, 'cept this here quarter. Show him the quarter, there.

PETERSON

Both of you — put up your hands and come over here.

STREETSINGER

Can't do that, suh — we's blind as bats, the both of us. Cain't one lead th' othuh; we cain't see where you is. We just singin' songs, mistuh. *(Sings with the old man playing the flute — there is something desperate about their singing now.)*

>So keep on sayin' it's the merriest,
>The best things in life —

73

PETERSON

Shut up. (*Peterson shines his flashlight into their faces.*) All right, you're not him; go on; get out of here —

STREETSINGER

Yes suh; we goin'. (*Peterson goes to the* "PHONE"; *dials.*)

PETERSON

Chief, this is Peterson. I need men. Hundreds of men; fast; I need help. (*pause*) No; stop everyone. I want everyone arrested. (*pause*) Everyone; it's got to be everyone. I don't know who he is. He could be anyone. Get me some help here fast. (*Hangs up; looks around the stage for Phillip; enter the wounded soldier from early Act One. Peterson, seeing soldier, shouts.*) Stop where you are!

WOUNDED SOLDIER

Help me . .

PETERSON

Stop or I'll shoot!

WOUNDED SOLDIER

Help me. (*The soldier falls; Peterson bends over him; backs away.*)

PETERSON

He's dead. (*looks closely at the soldier again*) It's not deKoch, that's for sure. It couldn't be him. (*Suddenly the wounded soldier is on his feet; lunges at Peterson, yelling.*)

WOUNDED SOLDIER

I only asked you to help me! (*Peterson fires several shots; the soldier does not stop.*)

PETERSON

Get away from me! (*Peterson runs offstage; the soldier staggers off the other side. Again we hear Phillip's laugh, savage, grotesque. It lasts for a few seconds; then Peterson creeps back into the downstage area. Suddenly the lights come up upstage. There is the preacher and his band, from early Act One.*)

PREACHER

(*pointing at Peterson*) You!

PETERSON

(*with his gun drawn*) Hold it right there. Don't move.

PREACHER

Your guns are useless against a man of the Lord.

PETERSON

I can see right through you this time. Put up your hands, deKoch!

PREACHER

You seek someone?

PETERSON

Come down here.

PREACHER

Seek and ye shall find; what ye seek is in the Lord.

PETERSON

Disguises won't work anymore, deKoch.

PREACHER

There is no disguise from the Lord: we poor players have no masks from he who sees all. All, brother. (*The band groups around Peterson and plays "Nearer My God to Thee," leading Peterson upstage.*) Hallelujah, brothers; another sheep into the fold! (*They all exit; Peterson breaks away, comes back downstage. Phillip's evil laugh comes from the right. The inspector runs off to the right; Phillip's laugh comes from the left; Peterson reenters from the right. Then Peterson enters from the left. Peterson regards Peterson, and vice versa.*)

PETERSON ONE

Hold it right there. I've got you this time. What do you think you're doing?

PETERSON TWO

All right, deKoch; put up your hands; you can't get away this time.

PETERSON ONE

Impersonating a police officer and murder; you've had it, deKoch.

PETERSON ONE and **PETERSON TWO**

Throw down your gun or I'll shoot. (*They both shoot; they both fall. Silence. Phillip enters from upstage, lit by a follow-spot; he is in his King Lear costume. Lights fade on the stage except for follow-spot on Phillip; he comes full downstage. He begins his next lines very quietly; very intensely. As the speech progresses, it becomes less intense; a distinct note of joy enters in; by the end of the speech, Phillip is laughing the words; complete joy, affirmation, love.*)

PHILLIP

Blow, winds, and crack your cheeks! Rage! Blow!
You cataracts and hurricanes, spout
Till you have drench'd our steeples, drown'd the cocks!
You sulph'rous and thought-executing fires,
Vaunt-couriers of oak-cleaving thunderbolts,
Singe my white head! And thou, all-shaking thunder,
Strike flat the thick rotundity o' th' world!

DAVID BALL

Crack nature's moulds, all germens spill at once
That makes ingrateful man!
(*Phillip turns; Melissa is standing to his side. They regard each other for
a second; then they bow to each other, and the curtain falls.*)

Assassin! by David Ball opened December 5, 1968, at the
Theatre in the Round in Minneapolis, Minnesota. It was directed by James Wallace.

Cast of Characters

PHILLIP	Allan Karol
WOUNDED SOLDIER, BEGGAR, CUSTOMS OFFICER, COP	
	Bill Zweber
BARTENDER, ARMY OFFICER	Don Wahl
DOPE SELLER	Chris Forsland
PREACHER	Parker Congdon
FRANZ	Jeffrey B. McLaughlin
MELISSA	Sharon White
FIGURE ONE, PHONE LADY	Eddy Cohen
OLD MAN	John Grill
GYPSY	Nancy Grill
NATASHA	Fairlie Arant
JASON, GLOUCESTER, AGENT ONE	Joseph Praml
GENTLEMAN, COP	Bob Engels
EDGAR	Mathew Tombers
STREETSINGER, AGENT TWO	Mel Edman
GO-GO DANCER	Sarah O'Connor
GUNMAN	Dwight B. Hicks
PETERSON	Allan Shapiro
FIGURE TWO	Michael A. Robins
SECOND INSPECTOR	Harry Rapaport

SEYMOUR LEICHMAN

Freddie the Pigeon

A TALE OF THE SECRET SERVICE FEATURING
FREDDIE THE PIGEON, FELICIA DOILEY, AN
ANGEL WITH AN IDENTITY CRISIS, OTIS THE
CLOUD, AND VARIOUS VISUAL DEVICES

for Judith

Cast of Characters

THE SINISTER DR. SYDNEY, archvillain and international criminal

BLAYLOCK, the man in the imported Belgian touring cap

LITNESS, the man with wings

PLOTKIN

THE CATS

BLOSSALINDA, the princess with no part

OTIS THE CLOUD

FREDDIE THE PIGEON

JUDY ELLEN, his pigeon girl friend

SAM, the boy genius

QUENTIN, the Goody Two-shoes pigeon

FAIRY GODMOTHER

FELICIA DOILEY, the angel with an identity crisis

MR. BIRDWELL of the CIA

GRIMSBY, his secretary

MR. CHVIK, the ex-secret agent allergic to danger

MISS CLEAVER, MISS GOULD, MISS BOOTH, MISS BANDSAW, the pigeon feeders

NARRATORS and PIGEONS and CLOUDS and OTHER VOICES

FREDDIE THE PIGEON

A darkened stage houses a "monkey bar" set containing various levels and platforms. As music comes up film footage of clouds moves around the theatre ending at the highest platform on the stage. A slide of Otis the Cloud "supers" over an actor in white coveralls. A team of narrators, two men and a girl, appear onstage and stay during the entire action.

NARRATOR D

(*godlike voice*) All the clouds are beautiful. They are beautiful to look at, and then, when they rain, they help humanity. They disappear for a while, but then they become vapor and rise up to become clouds again. That is the life cycle.

NARRATOR M

Wait a minute, Dan.

NARRATOR D

What is it, Mike?

NARRATOR M

Something strange is going on up here

NARRATOR D

What is it, Mike?

NARRATOR M

We've got a cloud up here that refuses to rain.

NARRATOR D

A cloud that won't rain? Can you get close to him?

NARRATOR M

There seems to be a crowd of clouds gathering . . But this is the story of Otis, the cloud who would not rain.

CAST

Come on, Otis, do it!

OTIS

Nope.

CAST

But Otis, you have to become water sooner or later.

OTIS

Don't make waves.

NARRATOR M

And so Otis drifted — a dropout from the life cycle. (SLIDE) He was a phenomenon in scientific circles. Once he was given the keys to the city of Cincinnati, Ohio, for holding back the rain, enabling the Cincinnati Reds to win a crucial doubleheader and then win the pennant in 1961. (*The cast cheers.*) And he became extremely vain. (SLIDE)

OTIS

Why not? My role in life is to be beautiful and inspirational. I like things just the way they are. I can come and go as I please. Besides, I don't especially like people — for example — (*Below appear the Sinister Dr. Sydney, Litness, Blaylock, Plotkin, and the cats standing around Sam who is strapped to a table with electrodes here, there, and everywhere.*)

DR. SYDNEY

Why do you want to be difficult? Can't you see we are your friends? We want to help you! All you have to do, little boy, is relax your brain.

SAM

Never!

DR. SYDNEY

What do you want to be that way for? Nobody likes a sore loser. Come on, little boy, what do you say?

SAM

Never! I am true to the red, white, and blue!

BLAYLOCK

You want I should lean on him, chief?

DR. SYDNEY

Let's dispense with this talk of leaning, Blaylock! No *leaning*! After all, we are not barbarians. But we have ways to make you talk. (*to Sam*) What's your favorite ice cream?

SAM

Butter pecan.

DR. SYDNEY

Miss Plotkin.

PLOTKIN

Yes, chief.

DR. SYDNEY

Butter pecan. (*She produces a half-gallon of ice cream. Dr. Sydney begins to drop all manner of colored capsules in it.*) You like butter pecan, don't you, Litness? All our boys get the very best treatment. (*Blossalinda, the princess with no part, enters from above. She wears a "Grimm's" princess gown and clutches lilies to her bosom.*)

BLOSSALINDA

Save me! Save me!

SAM

Why?

BLOSSALINDA

I'm in danger.

SAM

You're not in danger.

BLOSSALINDA

Are you sure? (*Sam nods yes.*) Oh. (*exits*)

DR. SYDNEY

. . uh, all our boys get the very best treatment.

SAM

Never!

DR. SYDNEY

Never, never, never, never, never, young man, is a very long time. Look, look what a beautiful day it is. Look at the sky. Look at the clouds. Look at the colored TV. And these nice cats to play with.

SAM

But I don't like cats.

BLAYLOCK

Come on, chief, let me lean on him.

OTIS

Why should I rain? They don't deserve it. That's the Kingdom of Grumbalyn.

CAST

What's a Grumbalyn? (SLIDE)

NARRATOR A

That's a Grumbalyn.

NARRATOR D

That's a Grumbalyn.

NARRATOR M

That's a Grumbalyn.

NARRATOR A

That is a place where practically no one ever says "thank you," and no one, but *NO ONE* ever says, "You're welcome." They spend six months out of the year keeping people off the grass.

VOICE ONE

Hey you!

VOICE TWO

Nobody likes a wise guy.

VOICE THREE

If I told you once, I told you a hundred times!

VOICE FOUR

You want to make something out of it?

NARRATOR A

They have names like Knuckles . .

NARRATOR M

. . and Red . .

NARRATOR D

. . and Sloppy Joe . .

NARRATOR A

. . and Ronald . .

CAST

Ronald?

NARRATOR A

And they never go to the dentist. They spend the first six months of the year keeping people off the grass and making signs which begin with . .

CAST

NO!

NARRATOR A

Then every June they have their annual beer festival, because Grumbalyns love their beer, and they turn into most dreadful bullies. (MOVIE: *Beer in ten-foot steins filling up and slopping over. Cut to riot footage.*)

NARRATOR D

And like all bullies, they are stupid and quick to argue.

NARRATOR M

If they can't argue with strangers, they argue with themselves.

NARRATOR D

Then they rumble and grumble and break windows and furniture and it's a frightful place, just frightful.

FREDDIE THE PIGEON

NARRATOR M

Then, when all the windows in Grumbalyn are broken and smashed up, lo and behold it is New Year's Eve and they start keeping people off the grass again.

NARRATOR A

A frightful place, just frightful. (*end of slide and movie sequence*)

NARRATOR D

Grumbalyn was the headquarters of that international conspirator, master of intrigue, and archvillain, the Sinister Dr. Sydney.

DR. SYDNEY

Nothing stops me, because I stop at nothing.

NARRATOR D

He made his headquarters in the maze. (SLIDE: *Maze.*)

PLOTKIN

A maze is a place that is very easy to enter, but almost impossible to get out of. The walls are so high that you never know where you are. If you ever get stuck in it, you are doomed to wander forever. There the lost children wandered endlessly, almost making contact but not quite.

NARRATOR D

Because the Sinister Dr. Sydney, from his hidden control panel, could control the walls at will. It was a cruel game.

DR. SYDNEY

But it keeps them on their toes.

NARRATOR D

It was the place that the Sinister Dr. Sydney kept lost boys. Posing as a kindly child psychologist, he specialized in day dreamers.

SAM

(*still strapped to the table*) And mathematical geniuses.

NARRATOR D

He stole them, brainwashed them, and sold them to foreign countries. All countries bought from him. Even we did.

BLAYLOCK

I don't understand, chief; if we kidnap the kid, why don't we just sell him back to his own mother and father?

DR. SYDNEY

Blaylock! You missed the point entirely. We are responsible for maintaining the balance of mathematical geniuses in the world. You cannot have a German mathematical genius working in Germany. He must defect to the U.S. An American mathematical genius must defect to the Soviet Union.

So it goes. Blaylock, I am afraid you have no head for business. Miss Plotkin!

PLOTKIN

Yes, chief.

DR. SYDNEY

Get me Chairman Mao in China.

PLOTKIN

Yes, chief.

DR. SYDNEY

(*on phone*) Ahhhh! My dear Chairman, hun me chung ding ding. How wow brown cow sini wakka ding ding. That's right, Mr. Chairman, chinky chose always shows. (*hangs up*) You see, Blaylock, we get infinitely more money dealing with foreign powers.

BLAYLOCK

I still don't like it, chief. It's un-American.

DR. SYDNEY

By the way, Blaylock, what's that after-shave lotion you use?

BLAYLOCK

It's called Dirt.

PLOTKIN

He seems to be coming around, chief.

DR. SYDNEY

Observe, Blaylock. (*Plotkin produces an atomizer and sprays Dr. Sydney's throat.*)

SAM

Where am I?

DR. SYDNEY

Why hello there, little man.

SAM

Where am I? And how did I get here?

BLAYLOCK

We're here to brainwash you.

DR. SYDNEY

Blaylock!

OTIS

The plot thickens! (*The stage blacks out. When the lights come up we are at what appears to be a fashion show. It is graduation day at Fairy Godmother Conservatory. Yes, there is such a place. Fairy Godmother descends the stairs. She is a generously proportioned Nordic type. Flowing hair or thick braids are optional.*)

FREDDIE THE PIGEON

NARRATOR A

And now, for the ladies, definitely of our age, or any age, a poetic fusion of the timely and timeless. Fairy Godmother is a vision in a full-length, cloud-soft, silk tissue gauze creation, kissed all over in a pattern of triumph tulips in the snow.

FAIRY GODMOTHER

Stu-dents, those of you who leave our hallowed halls today embark upon a career of miracles and good works. Your final examination has been carefully prepared by the very best minds here at Fairy Godmother Conservatory. Remember that you follow in the footsteps, or wingsteps, whichever the case may be, of an illustrious tradition. When Snow White vanquished the Wicked Witch, we were there. When the Princess was freed from Rumpelstiltskin, we were there. And let us not forget who took Cinderella to the ball! Yes, we were there and you who graduate from here today ensure the fact that we will always be there, wherever and whenever we are needed. (*applause*) First finalist, Miss Felicia Doiley. (*Felicia steps forward.*)

NARRATOR A

Miss Doiley's maxi-jersey connotes the reckless free spirit. Wings are a Rudi Gurnreich original — pliant, crushable, soft as rain, and the perfect footnote to Miss Doiley's ensemble, lavender plush spats by Columbo of Sicily, featuring the walking — or if you will, flying — heel. (*Two cast members sit at Felicia's feet. They are pumpkins.*)

FAIRY GODMOTHER

Don't be nervous, my child. All right: Part I. Pumpkins into coach. (*Felicia raises her training wand. It is all chewed up.*) My dear, what have you done to your training wand?

FELICIA

Well, it helps me to concentrate.

FAIRY GODMOTHER

(*gently*) Now, there must be no more of that. Remember, a sound training wand is essential for casting a good spell. All right then, let us begin, shall we? Pumpkin into coach. Left to right.

FELICIA

Pumpkin into coach. That's left to right, pumpkin into coach.

FAIRY GODMOTHER

Very well, then, begin.

BLOSSALINDA

Save me! Save me!

FAIRY GODMOTHER

Blossalinda, you are not in this scene — you're not even in this play.

BLOSSALINDA

Are you sure?

FAIRY GODMOTHER

I'm positive.

BLOSSALINDA

Oh! (*Felicia goes right to left and casts the spell on a downstroke, vigorously.*)

FAIRY GODMOTHER

No, no, no, my dear. It's pumpkin into coach, not pumpkin into mice. It's mice into horses.

FELICIA

I am sorry, pumpkin into mice, mice into horses, horses into pumpkin.

FAIRY GODMOTHER

No, no, pumpkin into coach, mice into horses.

FELICIA

It certainly is a whole lot to keep straight. (*They are waving together now.*)

FAIRY GODMOTHER

(*gently*) Let's begin again, shall we? Pumpkin into coach, mice into horses . .

FELICIA

(*equally gently*) Pumpkin into coach, mice into horses, horses into mice, coach into pumpkins. (*raises wand*)

FAIRY GODMOTHER

No, no, no, you are up too high! (*Felicia begins downstroke.*) You are striking too fast! (*Puff of pink smoke; horses, mice, coach, everything disappears and a four-foot flamingo-red French fried potato appears on stage.*)

OTIS

I don't believe it.

FAIRY GODMOTHER

That is NOT the assignment!

FELICIA

But isn't it a terrific color?

FAIRY GODMOTHER

My dear child, in the long, illustrious history of Fairy Godmother Conservatory, no one has ever, that is to say . . in all my years . . to put it more precisely, I am not sure that you are suited for this line of work.

FELICIA

Oh, Fairy Godmother, please! It's only the logistics that get me all confused. You must admit I'm terrific on execution.

FAIRY GODMOTHER

I am afraid it is hopeless, my child. After all, there are certain things that are basic. This is a wand, not a weapon.

FELICIA

But, Fairy Godmother . . !

FAIRY GODMOTHER

I am sorry, Felicia. It is my regrettable duty to inform you . .

FELICIA

Don't expel me. Please. What will I do with my wings?

FAIRY GODMOTHER

That, my dear, is not our concern. Perhaps in another year . .

FELICIA

But, Fairy Godmother . .

FAIRY GODMOTHER

There, there, my child. Remember, many are called, but few are chosen. (*Fairy Godmother taps herself with her own wand. Puff of smoke. Disappears. Everything disappears. Felicia is alone on the stage.*)

FELICIA

Why can't I manage something like that? (*putting on her wings*) Oh, well, you can't cry over spilled mice — and a stitch in nine gathers no moss.

OTIS

I don't believe it.

FELICIA

Will I never learn to curb my high spirits? Yet somehow I feel I must manage not to be discouraged. After all, does one require a diploma to do good works? (*Starts flying. Clouds move very quickly behind her as she is in stationary position flapping her wings.*)

OTIS

She's crazy! Look at her go.

FELICIA

(*sings "Indian Love Call" while flying out over the audience*) OOOOOOO.

OTIS

Hey, look out. Look out! (*Felicia, still singing, approaches Otis.*) Look out, look out!! (*point of contact*) I knew it. Oooooooh!!!

FELICIA

Ohhhh! Did I hurt you?

OTIS

Ooooooohhh! Rockets I can take. Airliners I can take, but, madam, those are very sharp wings.

FELICIA

It's just not my day I guess.

OTIS

I know.

FELICIA

You saw?

OTIS

Yep.

FELICIA

Well, it *is* an awful lot to keep straight in your head.

OTIS

You were terrible.

FELICIA

Don't remind me.

OTIS

Stop chewing on your wand. Didn't the lady tell you not to chew on that?

FELICIA

I really had my heart set on becoming a Fairy Godmother.

OTIS

Well, kid, you can't win 'em all.

FELICIA

I suppose it is better to have loved and lost than to look for the silver lining.

OTIS

What do you mean?

FELICIA

Well, look at me! These wings and this harp and this wand. You'd think I would be a natural. Instead I've got an identity crisis. By the way, my name is Felicia.

OTIS

Otis the Cloud. Charmed. (SLIDE)

FELICIA

Hey, it's terrific up here! You mean you can just stay here in one spot if you like?

OTIS

Sure!

FELICIA

Boy, you're lucky. Hovering in one place is the hardest thing for me to do.

OTIS

Take off your wings. Relax. Loosen your girdle.

FELICIA

I don't wear a girdle.

OTIS

You know what I mean. I mean stop worrying. So you flunked, so what!

FELICIA

But it was my destiny!

OTIS

Destiny, schmestiny. There's no such thing.

FELICIA

Everyone has a destiny. Everyone and everything on earth is meant for something.

OTIS

How tiresome.

FELICIA

Well, that's just the way it is.

OTIS

Not if you play your cards right!

FELICIA

I don't play cards.

OTIS

That is not what I mean. Take me for instance! Now I named myself after the Otis Elevator Company. The only difference is they go up and down and I only go up. I like to take life easy. I like to roll out there on a sunny day, head south for the winter.

FELICIA

Go south for the winter? Gee, a cloud that won't rain.

OTIS

That's right. I will not rain. Nor will I drip, rumble, or have anything to do with any, I repeat, *any* atmospheric disturbance.

FELICIA

But what do you do?

OTIS

In short, madam, nothing. I am a philosopher.

FELICIA

Talk about depth!

OTIS

Yes, my child, from this vantage point you will learn that all life is a stage on which are played a million dramas daily. (*sound effect: beep, beep, beep, beep.*)

FELICIA

What's that?

OTIS

That, my dear, is a drama heading our way. (*Freddie circles audience.*)

FELICIA

Gee! It looks like a pigeon to me! Hi.

OTIS

Hi.

FREDDIE

Hi. (*cough, cough*) Ohh! This air pollution is very bad today. (*cough*)

FELICIA

Hey, what are those things attached to your legs?

FREDDIE

Well, the left leg is my message capsule. And that thing on my right leg is my electronic radar homing device. They weigh a ton.

FELICIA

Well, why do you wear them?

FREDDIE

Because I'm a secret agent.

OTIS and FELICIA

Secret agent?

FREDDIE

Pigeon division.

OTIS and FELICIA

Pigeon division?

FREDDIE

It's a long story.

OTIS

We got plenty of time.

FELICIA

Oh, yes!

FREDDIE

A little flashback music, please! (*music*)

NARRATOR D

(*reading from title page of book*) Freddie the Pigeon. A tall tale of the secret service. Accounting how Sam, the mathematical genius, encounters

Characters from the Play

SEYMOUR LEICHMAN, ARTIST

Freddie the pigeon

Felicia
Doiley
&
Otis the Cloud

Plotkin, Blaylock, Litness & The Sinister Dr. Sydney

Mr. Churik is allergic to danger

Miss Cleaver   Miss Booth   Miss Bandsaw

the Sinister Dr. Sydney and his forces of darkness, in a rousing adventure of suspense and international intrigue, threatening the fate of the entire free world. (*Pigeons in the Park sequence. The following is to be interspersed with music. We are in a city park, Freddie's home turf. Three ladies enter wearing tennis sneakers and carrying shopping bags and umbrellas. Then pigeons enter, perhaps a cat or two chase them, see the ladies, then run off.*)

MISS BOOTH

Did you have a good night's sleep, honey?

MISS CLEAVER

Well, yes. But I could have sworn there was a Communist under my bed. I poked around till one in the morning.

MISS BANDSAW

I got to get a new pair of sneakers.

MISS BOOTH

Would you like a piece of Tootsie Roll?

MISS GOULD

I can't, honey. My new dentures just couldn't stand it.

MISS BOOTH

What do you want to do today?

MISS GOULD

Feed the birds.

MISS BANDSAW

No. Let's go down and picket the zoo.

MR. CHVIK

Good morning, ladies.

ALL

Good morning, Mr. Chvik.

MR. CHVIK

I trust you slept well?

MISS GOULD

I didn't.

MR. CHVIK

Oh?

MISS GOULD

There was a leak in my hot water bottle. And then early this morning I took it downtown for a refund and that salesman told me it was seven years old — and he wouldn't give me a refund.

MR. CHVIK

How unfortunate. What did you do?

91

MISS GOULD

I gave him some of this, deary. (*shakes her umbrella*) And you had better believe it.

MISS BANDSAW

Here, Quentin. Nice Quentin.

MISS GOULD

Freddie, you just can't burn the candle at both ends.

ALL THE LADIES

Why can't you be more like Quentin?

JUDY ELLEN

That's all right, Freddie. (*Quentin takes their birdseed and warms up to the ladies.*)

FREDDIE

(*to audience*) Why don't I eat their birdseed? I'll tell you why I don't eat their birdseed. Because it tastes like an old lady's purse. That's why I don't eat their birdseed. (*Miss Bandsaw gives Freddie Hartz Mountain Birdseed. Freddie spits.*) Lint! (*The music continues — and Sam feeds the pigeons. The cats have come and gone.*)

NARRATOR D

Up on the roof of his apartment building, Sam, Freddie's best friend, had built a coop which could only be locked from the inside, so that Freddie could come and go as he pleased. It was a good friendship as friendships go, because they respected each other's privacy. (*The music continues.*)

MR. CHVIK

What's new today, Sam?

SAM

Nothing new, Mr. Chvik, but I find that I have to reevaluate my equation as it relates to the velocity of my new atomic fuel.

MR. CHVIK

Oh?!

NARRATOR D

Yes, Sam was a mathematical genius. This was discovered at the breakfast table one morning when Sam's mother inquired:

SAM'S MOTHER

Will you have some formula?

SAM

(*in diapers*) XYZ squared plus ten squared equals ten XYZ to the fourth power.

NARRATOR D

Because he was a good deal brighter than most boys and girls his age . .

LITTLE GIRL

Two plus two is four.

SAM

X squared plus Y squared equals XYZ squared.

NARRATOR D

Sam took to being alone most of the time. Not that he was unfriendly. It was just that they did not share the same interests. And so, as Sam grew older and further apart from his classmates, he became friendlier with Freddie the Pigeon. (*The music continues.*) But Freddie was not his own bird. (*Enter the Sinister Dr. Sydney and entourage. The cats who had tyrannized the birds join the Sinister Dr. Sydney, Plotkin, Litness, and Blaylock. They surround Sam and kidnap him. Fade out as kidnapping occurs.*)

FREDDIE

Once I was a happy pigeon. Free as the air.

NARRATOR D

Yes; once he was a happy pigeon, free as the air.

FREDDIE

I said that!

NARRATOR A

As pigeons go, Freddie was nothing fancy any more. (*Enter Misses Booth, Cleaver, Bandsaw, and Gould.*) On cold, damp mornings his wings ached. Air pollution had cut his wind drastically, and if you took one whiff of him you did not want to take another.

FREDDIE

I resent that.

MISS CLEAVER

Freddie, you're a sight.

FREDDIE

You got a bromo?

MISS BANDSAW

(*to Miss Booth*) It happens every time he eats the leftover chocolate off the Good Humor sticks.

FREDDIE

Ohhh! My stomach is killing me. Listen, lady, maybe you got a Tums for the tummy?

MISS GOULD

What do you expect when you stay out all night eating pastrami . .

MISS BOOTH

And pizza . .

MISS BANDSAW

And herrings in wine sauce.

MISS CLEAVER

Here, Freddie, this stuff is better for you than that garbage you keep picking up.

QUENTIN

You know, Freddie, if you did fifty pushups a day you would be a new pigeon in no time.

FREDDIE

What a Goody Two-shoes. Knock it off, Quentin.

QUENTIN

Freddie, why be unsociable?

FREDDIE

I'm wise to that teacher's pet routine of yours. I just don't trust that bird.

MISS GOULD

He is absolutely right. Look at how healthy Quentin is.

MISS BANDSAW

Look at how nicely he eats.

FREDDIE

How could I play it like Quentin? I mean, sooner or later a pigeon has to make a decision — about — call it style. Now me, I'm a high stepper, a big spender — love 'em and leave 'em. You know what I mean?

JUDY ELLEN

Freddie. Freddie. Where were you? I waited up half the night.

FREDDIE

You know how it is, kid. *Yellow Submarine* was playing over at the Radio City Music Hall.

FELICIA

(*upstairs*) Hey, Freddie, how come you could go to the movies?

FREDDIE

It's simple. I'm a pigeon, right? While the ticket takers are taking tickets from the people, I just walk in, sneak in under a seat; there's all the popcorn I could ever ask for, not to mention the Rockettes.

NARRATOR M

Yes, Freddie loved the movies and spent many pleasant afternoons at the Radio City Music Hall.

FREDDIE

I said that!

FELICIA

Then how did you become a secret agent?

NARRATOR D

And Freddie loved his friends in the park.

NARRATOR M

And his sweetheart, Judy Ellen.

FELICIA

But how did he become a secret agent?

NARRATOR M

Why then did he have to give up the life he cherished . .

JUDY ELLEN

And the pigeon he loved?

NARRATOR A

To become a secret agent?

FELICIA

I just asked you that!

NARRATOR M

What were the forces that so conspired . .

CAST

Ooooooooooooh!

FELICIA

Conspired?

CAST

Ooooooooooooh!

NARRATOR M

What were the forces that so conspired, that sent him out into a life in the cold? You may well ask.

FELICIA

I just did.

NARRATOR M

It all began one day (SLIDE) when the American ambassador found that his phone was tapped. He was overheard by the other side. (SLIDE) The following day the Russian ambassador heard a suspicious tick in his tea-bag. (SLIDE) The English ambassador discovered an even smaller one in his molar (SLIDE), and his dentist, the world-famous Dr. Theodore Grib-bitz, was given twenty-four hours to leave the country. He worked, of course, for the other side. Within a week, all telephones were tapped. There were hidden microphones and tape recorders everywhere and every-body knew everybody else's top-secret plans. (SLIDE: *"We're bugged."*)

CAST

We're bugged!!!

NARRATOR M

Secrets agents everywhere were closing down shop. Who needs secret agents when there are no secrets. Double 07 took to drink and Monroe Zelinsky, alias the Red Shadow, became a volley-ball instructor. The capitals of the world were in an uproar. The CIA opened up a chain of launderettes to help cover expenses. The telephone tap became the latest craze to sweep the nation.

GIRLS

(*singing and dancing*)

> We've got zam!
> And we've got zap!
> We're doin'
> The Telephone Tap!

NARRATOR D

There was no doubt about it, everyone was bugged! Everyone knew the other side was to blame and they were right, of course, because to each the other was the other side. (SLIDE: *"We're bugged."*)

CAST

We're bugged!!!

NARRATOR D

And who was behind these sinister machinations? Who was making a fortune in the electronic-bugging-device business?

NARRATOR M

None other than the Sinister Dr. Sydney.

DR. SYDNEY

I'm just trying to turn an honest dollar.

NARRATOR M

One evening Sam and Mr. Chvik . .

FELICIA

Hey, wait a minute. Who's Mr. Shwick?

MR. CHVIK

That's Chvik!

FELICIA

Who's Mr. Shvik?

MR. CHVIK

That's Ch-vik!!! (*Enter Blossalinda.*) Not now, sweetheart.

FELICIA

But who are you?

MR. CHVIK

A little flashback-flashback music please. (*music*)

96

FREDDIE THE PIGEON

Once I was a master spy.
Danger was my game.
I'd triple cross a double cross
For trouble was my name.

    FELICIA

I thought it was Shvik.

    MR. CHVIK

I don't want to have to tell you again!!!
There was Tura in Warsaw in '29. Melzinki in Helsinki in '31. Von Krup-
    stock in Vladivostok in '33. Nobody ever got the best of me —
In Russian
In Prussian
In any espionage discussion.
When a master of duplicity
Was needed
They pleaded
For me!
When Von Benna of Vienna
Crossed the border to Ravenna
With a lettah
A vendetta
Against Hubert of Herzogovania —

    CAST

Herzogovania?

    MR. CHVIK

Yes!
Who was there to even up the score?

    CAST

You don't mean it?

    MR. CHVIK

I do!
I do!
It's true!
It's true!
. . And there's more!

    CAST

Do tell.

    MR. CHVIK

I shan't forget the night
When I dropped out of sight

To photograph some papers at the Embassy . .
Being where I was not
Supposed to be . .
Was my specialty.
Thinking myself alone in the room
I tiptoed softly through the gloom
When at once I heard a footfall on
The stair.
Patiently I held my breath and waited —

CAST

And waited . .

MR. CHVIK

And waited . .

CAST

And waited . .

MR. CHVIK

And waited . .

FELICIA

What happened???

MR. CHVIK

I thought you'd never ask.
That was the moment that changed my life.

CAST

Go on.

MR. CHVIK

If you insist.
I was not alone and
I knew that he knew —
And he knew that I knew
That he knew —
We stood facing each other
In the dark.
I thought to make my way through
The French doors to the courtyard
Below.
Inch by inch I inched my way along —
Oh . . I can't go on . .

CAST

Go on!

MR. CHVIK

It's too humiliating.

FELICIA

What happened!?!

MR. CHVIK

I sneezed!
And sneezed!
And once again I sneezed!
Achoo, achoo, achoo, achoo, achoo.
I died inside,
But it would not subside.
Achoo, achoo, achoo, achoo, achoo —
I was unmasked —
Betrayed by my own nose —

FELICIA

Mother of mercy!!!

MR. CHVIK

It was curtains for Mr. Chvik.

FELICIA

You don't mean . . ?

MR. CHVIK

Yes. I had become allergic to danger!
Betrayed by my own nose —
My sneeze was known everywhere.
I was finished as a secret agent.
The news spread like wildfire.
My double identity was kaput.

NARRATOR A

Yes, whenever he got in a tight squeeze
He'd sneeze.

MR. CHVIK

They know that already!

NARRATOR D

And so, because he was no good as a spy any more, they had to let him go.

NARRATOR M

He retired to Riverside Park to live amongst the forgotten people and feed the pigeons. One evening Sam and Mr. Chvik and Freddie were watching Huntley and Brinkley and found out all about the tap gap.

MR. CHVIK

I've got an idea. Let's give them Freddie.

SAM

What do you mean?

MR. CHVIK

Well, there's an old saying in the espionage game: "You can't bug a pigeon."

SAM

Gee, I never heard that.

MR. CHVIK

Oh, sure! We used to say it all the time. If pigeons carried messages in the old days before electronics, why can't they do it again? Freddie is an intelligent pigeon. How about it, Freddie? Don't you want to do something to help out?

FREDDIE

What has my country ever done for me, except to put up "Don't Feed the Pigeons" signs in the park? If it wasn't for you and Ladies' Aid, I would starve to death.

SAM

Freddie! I'm surprised at you. When I grow up I am going to serve my country as a mathematical genius on atomic projects for IBM.

MR. CHVIK

Ask not what your country can do for you, ask what you can do for your country.

NARRATOR D

There was no arguing with that, so it was decided right then and there. The idea really caught on. And a grateful nation gave Sam three days off from school.

NARRATOR A

A medal.

NARRATOR M

And a handshake from the president of the United States.

NARRATOR D

Chvik was given a Senior Citizen's Award for good citizenship, though the CIA declined, with thanks, his offer to head up the special pigeon project. The CIA closed down their chain of launderettes and were back in business. And one by one all the countries took it up until they all had their own unbuggable courier pigeons.

CAST

We're not bugged any more!
We've closed the tap gap!

FELICIA

Wow! Criminentlies!

OTIS

Criminentlies???

FELICIA

So that's how it happened?

FREDDIE

Wait. There's more! (*An office: red, white, and blue phones.* SLIDES: *radar screen and homing device chart. On desk: a name plate — "Mr. Birdwell. CC 1 Pigeon Division."*)

MR. BIRDWELL

Gentlemen, you will find that I run a very tight coop.

QUENTIN

Yes, sir!

MR. BIRDWELL

You are no longer Freddie and Quentin; you (*pointing at Freddie*) are CC 3, or if you wish, double C 3: C for Champion, C for Courier, 3 for 3. Quentin, you are CC 2. We do not speak unless we give the secret password. We do not shake hands unless we give the secret handshake. Indeed, we do not even enter this office unless we give the secret knock — or if we are pigeons, the secret scratch. Attached to your left leg you will find your message capsule — and attached to your right leg is your electronic homing device. When you are aloft and the fate of the free world is flying with you (*"America the Beautiful" begins*), we shall be able to record your whereabouts on this radar screen (*points to screen*). See Figure 2. (SLIDE) In short, we shall know precisely where you are at all times. Do I make myself clear, gentlemen?

FREDDIE

We are not gentlemen.

MR. BIRDWELL

I beg your pardon?

FREDDIE

I said we are not gentlemen. We are pigeons.

MR. BIRDWELL

Another red mark on your permanent record card. You have failed to give the password. CC 2, kindly demonstrate.

QUENTIN

(*rises*) "When it's apple blossom time in Orange, New Jersey . ."

MR. BIRDWELL

"We will make a peach of a pear." Well, then, off you go — my fine-feathered friends (*is fixing message capsules*) — and remember: the fate of the free world flies with you! (*music up and out*)

NARRATOR M

Freddie hated Mr. Birdwell.

FREDDIE

You can say that again.

NARRATOR M

Freddie hated Mr. Birdwell. Indeed, there is no meaner master than a minor civil servant.

FREDDIE

(*with Felicia and Otis*) The fate of the free world flies with you! Do you know what we carry in these message capsules? I've got a goddamned (*bleep*) recipe for cherries jubilee that the American ambassador's wife is sending to the French ambassador's wife! Top secret my eye! (*bleep*) Well, it's been nice chatting with you but I have to deliver this (*bleep*) message. (*exits*)

FELICIA

Bitterness is retroactive, Freddie. Remember the Doiley family motto: To forgive is human, to err divine.

NARRATOR M

He flew high over the city. He thought it strange that he saw no heavy traffic in the sky.

DR. SYDNEY

Begin the countdown, Miss Plotkin. (SLIDE; *music*)

PLOTKIN

Five, chief. Four, chief. Three, chief.

NARRATOR M

Not even the sparrows were aloft.

PLOTKIN

(*not having lost rhythm*) Two, chief. One, chief. Fire! (*Litness is airborne. Music.*)

FREDDIE

Something is wrong! I usually see at least a group of starlings.

NARRATOR M

There was a speck in the sky getting larger and larger.

NARRATOR A

Freddie was in big trouble.

NARRATOR M

It was a pigeon hawk and it was closing fast. Freddie flew for his life.

102

FREDDIE THE PIGEON

FREDDIE

He is fast —

NARRATOR A

— thought Freddie —

FREDDIE

— and big! If he gets me out in the open, I'm a dead pigeon.

NARRATOR M

He flew through the tall buildings and in and out of windows. He had not lived his whole life in New York City for nothing. Finally, perched in an eave high above Riverside Drive, the Hudson River and the West Side Highway stretched out before him, he rested.

FREDDIE

I think I've lost him.

NARRATOR M

His plan was to wait until dark and then make his way back to headquarters. In an eave of the building directly across the street perched the pigeon hawk. He was a hunter and he could wait. Freddie soared into the clear — and the hawk was on him immediately. They wrestled and clawed and ruffled and turned high above the West Side Highway. Freddie's left wing was badly clawed. With his last ounce of strength, he wrestled free, but the pigeon hawk, in an effort to get at the secret message, with his powerful claws wrenched the electronic homing device from Freddie's leg. In a swoon of pain, Freddie fell to the earth, counting his life in seconds.

NARRATOR D

As luck would have it, Freddie fell kerplunk into the back seat of an open sports car heading north on the West Side Drive, toward the George Washington Bridge and Pompton Lakes, New Jersey.

BLAYLOCK

(*on intercom in car*) It worked. I got him, chief! It worked!

DR. SYDNEY

I will meet you at Rendezvous Point 7: and remember, Blaylock, no rough stuff. He must appear to be among friends. (*Music. Back in the maze. Sign: "Happydale Pigeon Farm."*)

FREDDIE

Where am I?

BLAYLOCK

(*in an imitation of Dr. Sydney*) Were you looking for this? (*Holds message capsule aloft. Pause. Freddie reacts.*) I found it when I was tending your wounds. (*Gong. Enter Sinister Dr. Sydney and group.*)

DR. SYDNEY

Ah! My dear Blaylock, I see you have succeeded.

BLAYLOCK

He's all yours, chief.

DR. SYDNEY

Excellent! He shall make a most promising subject.

BLAYLOCK

And if he doesn't cooperate, he shall make an excellent dinner for the cats. (*The cats purr.*)

DR. SYDNEY

Put him in the cage with the other new arrival; then we can begin. (*Freddie is put into the cage with Judy Ellen.*)

JUDY ELLEN

Freddie!

FREDDIE

But, Judy Ellen, what are you doing here?

JUDY ELLEN

I was captured by the Sinister Dr. Sydney. But, oh, you are hurt!

FREDDIE

Never mind that, what's this all about?

JUDY ELLEN

They are after every *champion* pigeon in town. They brainwash them into betraying the Homing Pigeon Oath and becoming double agents. They fly here first, the Sinister Dr. Sydney reads the message, puts it back, then lets us birds fly on our way. Don't you see? He gets the information coming and going and sells it to the highest bidder.

DR. SYDNEY

Diversification is the key to industrial growth. (SLIDE) Here we brainwash the children. (SLIDE) Here we brainwash the pigeons.

FREDDIE

I thought you said that the Sinister Dr. Sydney was only after champion birds. What are you doing here?

JUDY ELLEN

I am not the dumb bird you took me for. I am, in fact, a graduate of Birdley, a true Seelenfreund. My ancestors flew the news across the English Channel during the Napoleonic Wars. (*Quentin flies over the maze.*) Look, Freddie, it's Quentin.

QUENTIN

Hi, Freddie, old pal.

FREDDIE

Don't old pal me, you double-crosser.

QUENTIN

You poor naive victims of the capitalist ruling class.

NARRATOR D

I think we can get down on the floor to Mike Kaplan who has Quentin the double agent — take it away, Mike.

NARRATOR M

Right, Dan.

NARRATOR D

Right, Mike.

NARRATOR M

Right, Dan.

QUENTIN

Hi, Mike, I've only got a minute. I've got to get this secret message to the Sinister Dr. Sydney.

NARRATOR M

The question on everyone's mind is how can you be a good guy and a bad guy in the same play?

QUENTIN

I just try harder, I guess.

NARRATOR M

What does it take to be a double agent?

QUENTIN

Strict training.

NARRATOR M

And what would you do if a third world power should want your services?

QUENTIN

If I can fit them in, why not?

FREDDIE

Right! He's a double agent. We've got to get out of here. (*Litness and Blaylock come for Freddie. He is strapped to a brainwash table.*)

DR. SYDNEY

This shouldn't be too difficult. After all we are dealing with a bird brain.

NARRATOR M

Although it was technically speaking an accurate appraisal of Freddie's faculties, he was nevertheless offended.

DR. SYDNEY

Ready, Miss Plotkin?

PLOTKIN

Ready, chief! (*She holds up capsule.*) Three Hartz Mountain Pigeon Yummies drenched in scopolamine.

DR. SYDNEY

Excellent, Miss Plotkin. (*to Freddie*) Now, my little winged friend, shall we begin? Red is blue and green is yellow and best is worst and sand is sea. I am such a friendly fellow that when you wake you'll work for me.

NARRATOR D

They kept this up for three days till Freddie was in a fog. They would not allow him to sleep.

DR. SYDNEY

Who are you?

FREDDIE

CC 3. That's me.

DR. SYDNEY

More Pigeon Yummies, Miss Plotkin.

NARRATOR A

Freddie hung on.

FREDDIE

Bird brain, am I? I must not give in. I must not give in!

NARRATOR D

But how long could he hold out? (*Enter Blossalinda.*)

BLOSSALINDA

Save me! Save me!

FREDDIE

Blossalinda, get out of here. This is my big scene. Here I am getting brain-washed by the Sinister Dr. Sydney and tortured by the cats and you come walkin' in on me. You can come in on Sam the mathematical genius, you can walk in on the Fairy Godmother, and you can walk in on Mr. Chvik — whatever his name is — but don't come in on me. For heaven's sake.

NARRATOR A

Oh, my dear, what a chic princess outfit — shroud gray.

BLOSSALINDA

Oh, do you really like it?

NARRATOR A

Oh, I love it.

DR. SYDNEY

Sam, do you like ice cream?

SAM

Yes.

DR. SYDNEY

Why not?

SAM

But I do like it, I do. I do like ice cream.

DR. SYDNEY

Why don't you like ice cream?

SAM

But I do, I do!

FELICIA

Gracious! Those people have terrible manners.

OTIS

I only like happy people with happy problems.

FELICIA

(*putting on her wings*) That's no way to treat a pigeon. And look down there in the maze.

DR. SYDNEY

(*standing over Sam*) Red is blue and green is yellow and best is worst and sand is sea. I am such a friendly fellow that when you wake you'll work for me.

PLOTKIN

Oh, chief! Can I try it once?!

DR. SYDNEY

Certainly not!

FELICIA

That poor little boy! That poor little pigeon. I have got to try to reach their friends in Riverside Park.

OTIS

You do-gooders are all alike.

DR. SYDNEY

(*to Freddie*) Beautiful little pigeon.

CATS

(*purring*) Beautiful little pigeon.

DR. SYDNEY

We are all civilized people.

FREDDIE

I'm not a people. I'm a pigeon. I've got to get some sleep.

DR. SYDNEY

Join us and you will have all the sleep you require.

CATS

(*with lust*) Beautiful little pigeon!

NARRATOR M

Meanwhile — back across the river, Felicia Doiley had made contact with Mr. Chvik.

MR. CHVIK

Aaaaachoooo!

FELICIA

I am certainly glad we made contact.

NARRATOR M

I said that.

MR. CHVIK

Aaaaaachooooo!

FELICIA

As you see, Freddie and Sam are in grave danger.

MR. CHVIK

Aaaachooo! Aaaaachoooo! I know, I know.

MISS GOULD

Where did you get the wings, honey?

MR. CHVIK

We have no time for that right now, my dear. There seems to be some sort of crisis. This kind lady . .

FELICIA

I am not sure I am a lady. I have an identity crisis.

MR. CHVIK

Let's take one crisis at a time.

MISS GOULD

Can you really fly, honey?

FELICIA

Yes. As a matter of fact, I can do a double barrel roll.

MR. CHVIK

Please, ladies, please! We must get organized!

FELICIA

Where did you get your sneakers?

MISS BANDSAW

Thom McAn.

MR. CHVIK

(*half to audience*) If I am not mistaken, the man who captured Freddie is none other than Vinton Blaylock, an operative of the Sinister Dr. Sydney.

LADIES

Sinister Dr. Sydney? Who's that?!

MR. CHVIK

That — aaaaachoooo — is a long story. We must go to the CIA at once.

MR. BIRDWELL

(*back in the* CIA *office*) Nonsense! I like a little intrigue as well as the next man, but this is clearly a hoax. You have already been decorated once by the president; don't try to make a good thing of it! And furthermore, if that bird Freddie ever does show his beak around here, it will surely be the last of him.

MR. CHVIK

Aaaaaachooooo!

FELICIA and LADIES

Gesundheit!

MR. BIRDWELL

Good day!

BLAYLOCK

(*back in the maze*) We are not getting anywhere, chief; he is recalcitrant.

DR. SYDNEY

Shhh! Wait.

PLOTKIN

He's coming around, chief.

FREDDIE

Cruel is kind and earth is sky. I have changed my mind. I will be your spy.

DR. SYDNEY

Excellent! He shall make a splendid double agent.

NARRATOR D

Refitting a duplicate message device and message capsule on Freddie, the Sinister Dr. Sydney replaces the now unsecret message.

DR. SYDNEY

Cherries jubilee?!

QUENTIN

Glad to have you on the team, Freddie.

FREDDIE

Happy to be here, dear friend, happy to be here.

DR. SYDNEY

(*aside to Quentin*) Quentin, you will accompany him in the event his brain is not completely washed.

JUDY ELLEN

Freddie! Freddie! What have they done to you?

FREDDIE

You poor naive victim of the capitalist ruling classes.

BLAYLOCK

Away all birds!

NARRATOR A

And so the birds flew low and fast over Pompton Lakes, New Jersey, heading south toward New York City.

FREDDIE

Why are we flying so low? We are just missing the trees!

QUENTIN

If we fly any higher we will be picked up on the radar screen of the CIA. They would be curious to know what we were doing in New Jersey, when we should be flying down Fifth Avenue. Pretty clever, eh?

NARRATOR M

Freddie looked up. Two hundred feet above flew Litness, the bird man. It would mean certain death to fly any higher.

PLOTKIN

The Sinister Dr. Sydney thinks of everything!

QUENTIN

Freddie, I'm glad you finally got wise to yourself.

FREDDIE

When did they brainwash you?

QUENTIN

They didn't have to. I volunteered. Hey, Freddie, what are you doing?!

NARRATOR A

Suddenly Freddie broke formation and started to climb.

QUENTIN

Freddie, what are you doing!?!?!?

FREDDIE

Putting you out of business. You won't be so popular with the CIA if your signal is picked up over Grumbalyn. And they will think it's your signal because they have given me up a long time ago. And, if you are no good to the CIA, you are no good to the Sinister Dr. Sydney. It's been nice knowing you.

NARRATOR M

Freddie flew to a hundred fifty feet, radar range for the CIA, did a double barrel roll just to make sure they got his signal, then dived for his life, the hawk in close pursuit. He had only one chance; he had to outrace Litness, the pigeon hawk, to his old coop (on top of Sam's building). If it was locked, he was finished. Once he had been clocked at sixty miles per hour in open competition, but that was a long time ago.

110

FREDDIE THE PIGEON

NARRATOR A

Besides, his left wing was still a mess.

NARRATOR M

Fifty feet behind zoomed the pigeon hawk, taking up the slack at a frightening rate. And fifty feet ahead was his coop. Freddie's lungs were bursting.

FREDDIE

My lungs are bursting.

NARRATOR A

If that coop wasn't open, he would be smashed to pieces on the wire mesh.

FREDDIE

Here goes!

NARRATOR M

It was open! He was in! It was shut and the pigeon hawk slammed into the mesh with a sickening jolt, bounced off, and fell dazed to the street below.

FREDDIE

(*to Chvik*) Quick, Chvik. Get this homing device off my leg and the message capsule. We haven't a moment to lose. In a few moments this place will be swarming with CIA men.

NARRATOR M

Meanwhile, back at the CIA.

GRIMSBY

(*picks up electronic "beep" message*) An electronic "beep" message near Grumbalyn, chief. Chief?

MR. BIRDWELL

What was that, Grimsby?

GRIMSBY

Chief, I just picked up . .

MR. BIRDWELL

Just a minute, Grimsby. Not without the password.

GRIMSBY

Roses are red . . ? My bonnie lies over the ocean . . ?

MR. CHVIK

(*flanked by Freddie and Felicia, addresses the ladies*) Are we to just stand here then while our little friend Sam is brainwashed in Grumbalyn?

MISS GOULD

You bet your bippy we ain't!

FELICIA

Come on, Otis, you can't hang back forever. Join us.

111

OTIS

I've got a pressing appointment, my dear . .

MISS BANDSAW

Onward then to great adventure and . .

MR. CHVIK

Aaaaaachooooo!

MISS BANDSAW

Danger! (*All exit to "Yankee Doodle Dandy."*)

NARRATOR A

And so our friends set forth for Grumbalyn to rescue Judy Ellen from the Happydale Pigeon Farm — and Sam from the Malevolent Maze. And now to Dan in Pompton Lakes, New Jersey.

NARRATOR D

Our little band of heroes parked in a secluded wood just outside of the Happydale Pigeon Farm near Pompton Lakes, New Jersey, in the land of Grumbalyn. Miss Gould produced a can of water paint and the ladies sprayed Freddie till he was the same color as Quentin. The result was amazing.

LADIES

Amazing!

NARRATOR D

Next they replaced the electronic device and message capsule on either leg.

MR. CHVIK

(*to Felicia and Freddie*) Make your way to the back fence of the pigeon farm. I'll give you ten minutes. Then the ladies and I will drive around to the front gate. You know what to do. Good luck!

NARRATOR D

Mr. Chvik produced an attaché case and, to Miss Cleaver's amazement, transformed himself into another person. Then he emptied the case of makeup and disguises and filled it with samples of birdseed.

NARRATORS A and M

Birdseed?

NARRATOR D

That's right, birdseed.

MR. CHVIK

Let's get started. When we get there, keep the motor running.

LADIES

Good luck, Mr. Chvik.

MR. CHVIK

(*whisper*) Aaachoo!

FREDDIE

(*to Felicia*) Look, there's Litness, Blaylock, and the cats!

FELICIA

(*standing up*) Hey, you're right. (*Freddie pulls her down.*) If we don't fool that hawk . .

FREDDIE

It's goodbye, Freddie.

FELICIA

Ready? Five . . four . . three . . two . . Go ahead, Freddie.

NARRATOR D

Freddie flew over the fence and headed straight for the landing block as Litness headed toward Freddie.

NARRATOR A

Felicia held her breath.

NARRATOR M

The cats did not stir.

ALL

It worked.

NARRATOR D

Felicia was under the fence in a flash and began her search for Judy Ellen.

MR. CHVIK

Hello there; my name is Menlo Dentish, your friendly Hartz Mountain representative.

DR. SYDNEY

Hello, my name is Harold Happydale.

MR. CHVIK

This month we are featuring our vitamin-packed Pigeon Peppy Pebbles.

DR. SYDNEY

Not interested.

MR. CHVIK

Mint flavored for sweeter breath, packed one hundred to a box.

DR. SYDNEY

I haven't got time right now.

MR. CHVIK

Individually packed in jet-age plastic for lasting freshness.

DR. SYDNEY

I am very busy, my good man.

MR. CHVIK

Each Peppy Pebble contains the minimum daily requirement your pigeon needs for firm coat, strong beak, sound bones.

NARRATOR A

Just as Felicia found Judy Ellen's cage, another bird flew over the fence with no place to go.

NARRATOR M

The real Quentin had returned!

NARRATOR D

The two birds stood face to face before an incredulous Blaylock.

BLAYLOCK

I'm incredulous.

NARRATOR D

He reasoned that one of them was an imposter.

BLAYLOCK

One of them is an imposter.

NARRATOR D

Snatching a bird in either hand, he crunched his way across the gravel yard and burst into the office where Harold Happydale was being engaged by Menlo Dentish.

DR. SYDNEY

Excuse me a moment, won't you?

MR. CHVIK

Certainly.

DR. SYDNEY

What is it, Mr. Smith?

NARRATOR D

Trapped in Blaylock's sweaty palm, Freddie's paint began to run.

DR. SYDNEY

Ah hah!

MR. CHVIK

Aachoo! (*pause*)

DR. SYDNEY

I would know that sneeze anywhere! Imposter, you are my archenemy, the mysterious Mr. Chvik.

MR. CHVIK

Drop that bird and stand where you are.

NARRATOR M

Unfortunately, Mr. Chvik . .

FREDDIE THE PIGEON

NARRATOR A

. . whose eyes were not what they were . .

NARRATOR M

. . in his hasty preparation had mistaken Sam's water pistol for his old service revolver. But quickly he squirted Litness squarely in the eye. The water pistol was loaded with carbonated, still-chilled, fresh 7-Up, a new invention among Sam's pals. It had sufficient fizz to force Litness to release both birds. (*Blaylock, Litness, and Sinister Dr. Sydney approach Chvik menacingly; Felicia and Freddie free Judy Ellen; sound of trumpet off-key; Miss Cleaver and Ladies' Aid to the rescue, flags flying, shopping bags flaying.*)

NARRATOR A

The villains were driven out into retreat into the gravel yard. The Sinister Dr. Sydney loosed Litness against Freddie, but Miss Cleaver whacked him into the middle of next Friday with her umbrella, while Freddie snatched the secret cherries jubilee recipe from the unsuspecting hand of Blaylock, managing to inflict heavy damage on his stunning imported Belgian touring cap.

MISS BANDSAW

Keep the pressure up, girls, they're giving ground.

DR. SYDNEY

Hurry, Blaylock, we must get to the control panel in the maze. (*Blaylock pulls gun, advances on Chvik; Felicia steps forward and transforms him into a flamingo-red French fried potato.*)

NARRATOR D

Meanwhile, back to Birdwell at CIA.

GRIMSBY

Green grow the lilacs? (*Birdwell as in charades makes an "a."*) Starts with — starts with "a." Avocado? Apricot? Anchovies? Apples?

BLOSSALINDA

(*whispers from behind Birdwell's back*) Blossoms!

GRIMSBY

When it's apple blossom time in Orange, New Jersey!!!

MR. BIRDWELL

It's about time, you nincompoop!

GRIMSBY

Sorry, chief, you have to give the countersign.

MR. BIRDWELL

We'll make a peach of a pear, you idiot!

DR. SYDNEY
(*at control panel*) From this control panel at least we can burn the little children to a crisp. (SLIDES) Miss Plotkin — throw the switch!

PLOTKIN
Chief, are you sure?

DR. SYDNEY
Just as I thought, Miss Plotkin. In moments of crisis you are betrayed by your femininity. (*pulls the switch himself; rumble in the maze as fire breaks out*)

CAST
(*ad libbing*) Fire! Fire! There's fire in the maze!

MR. CHVIK
Oh dear, the lost boys are lost! They will be burned to a crisp, every one of them. (MOVIE: *Lightning.*)

CAST
(*ad libbing*) Look! Up in the sky! It's a dirigible! It's a doughnut! It's Otis the Cloud!

OTIS
I've had a change of heart. For no good reason at all I've become a good guy!

FELICIA
Hurry up, Otis. The children will be burned to a crisp!

OTIS
I am hurrying. (*Thunder, rumbling. The stage goes blue.* FILM: *Snow.*)

NARRATOR D
Come on, Otis, rain!

CAST
That's not rain, it's snow!!! (*Snow falls all over. Otis on film fades away.*)

FELICIA
Don't go, Otis! Oh, don't go!

OTIS
You can't have it both ways, kid!

NARRATOR D
Yes, Otis the Cloud sacrificed himself for the people he loved and in so doing joined the life cycle.

FELICIA
Talk about sad! Otis? Where are you? Otis!?

OTIS
(*fading*) I'll be back.

116

FREDDIE THE PIGEON

DR. SYDNEY

Curses! Two of my operations destroyed in one day. (*The phone rings.*)
Ching chong finong, I'm sorry, Chairman, not now. (*hangs up*)

MISS GOULD

Look, he's getting away!

LADIES

(*ad libbing*) He's getting away!

DR. SYDNEY

You will rue the day you crossed the path of the Sinister Dr. Sydney. I will
reap revenge on the lot of you.

PLOTKIN

But, chief, what about me?

DR. SYDNEY

There is no room in my organization for weaklings. Off, Litness.

NARRATOR M

And the Sinister Dr. Sydney escaped . .

NARRATOR A

. . unexpectedly . .

NARRATOR D

. . on the wings of Litness. (*Quentin and the cats are tied to flamingo-red
French fried potato.*)

MR. CHVIK

Well, I guess that's that. (*Freddie and Sam embrace.*)

JUDY ELLEN

Oh, Freddie, you were wonderful!

FREDDIE

C'mere! (*She comes.*) Walk around me. (*She does.*) What'd you find?

JUDY ELLEN

I know — no strings. You don't have to worry, Freddie — I won't try to
hold you down. But remember (*seductively*) any time you want me, all
you have to do is whistle. You know how to whistle, don't you, Freddie?
Just pucker up and blow!

FREDDIE

We don't whistle — we're pigeons. We go burgle — burgle.

JUDY ELLEN

Oh yeah. I never thought of that.

MISS CLEAVER

I haven't had so much fun since we picketed the White House!

MR. CHVIK

Well, we all had better be getting along. I imagine the CIA will be here any minute now.

MISS BANDSAW

Gee! Sam, it's good to see you.

SAM

Oh, Miss Bandsaw, if it hadn't been for Freddie and all of you, I might be on my way to China.

MISS BOOTH

What are you going to do about Freddie?

LADIES

(*ad libbing*) Yes. What's going to happen to Freddie? Is he going back to the CIA?

SAM

I should say not! Just take a look at his left wing. If they don't know any better than to treat a bird that way, then they haven't any right to him.

MISS GOULD

We had better hurry, someone is coming. (*Mr. Birdwell discovers Sam's medal attached to the flamingo-red French fried potato.*)

MR. BIRDWELL

What's going on here? Why this is the president's medal to Sam! (*Plotkin enters.*) Who are you?

PLOTKIN

I am Miss Plotkin.

MR. BIRDWELL

What has happened here? We have been getting disturbance signals on the electronic radar homing device all afternoon. Miss . . Miss . . what did you say your name was?

PLOTKIN

(*removing glasses to clean them*) Plotkin!

MR. BIRDWELL

Why, Miss Plotkin, did anyone ever tell you, you were beautiful without your glasses? (*Chvik sneezes.*)

MISS BANDSAW

Is it danger, Mr. Chvik?

MR. CHVIK

No, just ragweed.

LADIES

God bless you. (*Felicia puts on her wings.*)

SAM

We don't know how to thank you, Miss Doiley.

FELICIA

Aw, it was nothing! Remember to forgive is human, to err is divine.

MR. CHVIK

Well, remember, there's always a place for you at Riverside Park and I'm sure I speak for all of us when I say . . Aaaaaachooooo!

FELICIA

(*with her wand*) God bless you!

ALL NARRATORS

PINNNNNNNGGGGGGG!!! (*a magic sound*)

MISS CLEAVER

What is it?

MR. CHVIK

It's my hay fever, it seems to have disappeared. It's a miracle!

CAST

It's a miracle!!!

FELICIA

The first spell I ever cast that wasn't a flamingo-red French fried potato! (*thunder*)

GOD

Doiley, Felicia! Number 74398! Welcome, you are my newest angel.

FELICIA

A promotion! I still don't know who I am, but one makes progress. (*She flies away. Otis reappears with clouds. The stage darkens.*)

Freddie the Pigeon by Seymour Leichman opened on August 12, 1969, at Playhouse in the Park, Cincinnati, Ohio. It was directed by Word Baker, with settings by Steve Carmichael, costumes by Caley Summers, props by Tom Oldendick, films by Robert Fries, slides by Robert Gerding, lighting by Lee Bonamy. The producer was Brooks Jones.

Cast of Characters

THE SINISTER DR. SYDNEY	Leigh Woods
BLAYLOCK	Bruce Fremont
LITNESS	Chris Weidenbacher
PLOTKIN	Judith Benjamin
THE CATS	Jaynie Katz, Cyndie Schatz, Bebe Rodman, Wendy Gradison
BLOSSALINDA	Robin Alexander
OTIS THE CLOUD	Tom Hummel
OTHER CLOUDS and OTHER VOICES	Michael Kaplan
FREDDIE THE PIGEON	Jon Fairbanks
SAM	Sam Garcia
QUENTIN	Tim Taylor
FAIRY GODMOTHER	Margo Skinner
JUDY ELLEN	Lucy Baker
FELICIA DOILEY	Penni Martin
MR. BIRDWELL	Eric Simon
GRIMSBY	Carolann Mary
MR. CHVIK	Andy Rohrer
MISS CLEAVER	Paula Gold
MISS GOULD	Kendell Fewell
MISS BOOTH	Connie McMahon
MISS BANDSAW	Michael Bass
NARRATORS and PIGEONS and OTHERS	Anita Trotta, Carol Doscher, Charlene Sprang

NANCY WALTER

Rags

Cast of Characters

POP

MOM

LUCY, their daughter

DRAVES, their son

THERESA, Draves's woman

RUBY, a relative

CLEMENT, a relative

The Setting

The only important set element is a pile of rags.

RAGS

PART ONE

1. *The theatre is dark for a change. We are thrown back upon the ear. The actors come into the dark separately. It is Draves's birth. The sounds of birth are made in the dark. Slowly at first and at regular intervals and then faster and louder and louder until the sounds are so close together they are one. Sudden light.*

MOM

It's him. It's a boy.

2. *Under the grape trees. In the near dark, Mom chooses her family and arranges them. Ruby, Theresa, and Clement stand outside the family circle and beckon to Pop, Draves, and Lucy to come out.*

MOM

I like it here, under the trees, out of the sun in the middle of the day. The wind is keeping the flies away.

POP

Your skin is too delicate for anything else. Not even the sun should distress you.

MOM

You've kept me from the darker things. You've sheltered me even from the sun. Look, my skin is still young.

POP

Still white.

LUCY

Pretty mother. What if I was your mother?

MOM

Then the world would be upside down.

LUCY

Pretty mother. The world is upside down.

MOM

Not here, under the trees, Everything is right.

DRAVES

Mother, can I put your head in my lap?

MOM

Yes, put your head in my lap. Take a little nap. Soon we'll go in.

LUCY

What if you were my little puppy?

POP

What if? What if?

MOM

Soon we'll go in. To eat. And to bed. Being out here under the trees has made us all sleepy.

LUCY

What if my tongue could reach you? (*silence*) What if my tongue were as long as all the trees put together?

POP

Get some sense in your head.

MOM

What would you do with it, Lucy?

LUCY

Grab onto heaven.

POP

This is heaven.

DRAVES

No, not this. There is more to heaven than this.

MOM

It only might be heaven.
Tell me more about your tongue. Tell me, Lucy,
What you want to reach with it.

LUCY

See? It doesn't reach very far. I can't touch anything with it. See?

DRAVES

See what? Around here.

POP
Not so much noise, son.

MOM
Sh sh sh. (*to Pop*) Put your head on my lap.

DRAVES
Put your head where it belongs.

POP
(*puts head down; Mom rubs his head*) O it feels good. Just this stroke is
so peaceful.
It's like before.
When there were only the two of us.

MOM
Like before.
When you'd come home to me so tired.

POP
But exhilarated
From putting things in order,
From saying harsh things,
From reaching as far as I could.
It wasn't easy.

MOM
I know you did it for us.

POP
Not enough. We must keep on making order.

LUCY
I want to make something too.

DRAVES
Not me. I want to take things apart.

MOM
Sh. Let's go inside.

DRAVES
It's too small in there. My head almost touches the ceiling. It's like a doll's
house. I can hear everything you do. And it doesn't smell good in there.

MOM
How can you say those things to me?

POP
You ought to be slapped.

MOM
Don't bother with that, dear. Lie down again.

125

LUCY
Lie down.
POP
No, I'm not ready to lie down. Not yet.
DRAVES
I'm not going in.
POP
Quit screaming.
LUCY
I would wrap my tongue around you so you couldn't get away. (*By now, Pop, Draves, and Lucy have gone to the tempters.*)
MOM
I'm not going away. I'm going inside. (*sings**)

> Ev'rything was inside
> The mother at first.
>
> She lets ev'ry kind of life
> Belonging to her go.
>
> She lets ev'ry kind of life go.
>
> The mother made rivers
> circles
> The mother made children
> heavens
>
> She lets ev'ry kind of life
> Belonging to her go.

3. *Pop's office.*

CLEMENT
You're the boss.
Whatever you do
Everyone will say it's good.
What more can you hope for?
You have to make up your mind. (*gestures toward Ruby about whom they speak as if he were not there*) He's from another culture.
But he'll stay in line, he'll have to.
POP
They tell me it's falling apart.

*The music for the songs is available from Nancy Walter, c/o Firehouse Theatre Co., 1572 California St., San Francisco, California 94109.

That our impulses are perverted
And frightened.
I have watchmen everywhere
And they tell me
That all over the country hands
Are clenched
Looking for something to hit.

CLEMENT

Why don't we just let nature take its course?

POP

Has it come to that?
Is it true that things are worse?
Just yesterday I thought they were better.
I know there isn't a promised land anymore
But the world grows old.
And I have loved this country
And felt it to be good
In spite of mistakes
Which I have tried to ignore.
It's fading and may still explode.

CLEMENT

Not if you take a hand in it.

POP

We must make things quiet.
We need to do nothing.
We need to put destruction to sleep
And let the sweet cement of peace heal us.
We have to insist on clarity
And if that involves personal sacrifice
We must make it and make others make it.
(*to Clement*) And you, you must go inside all over
And let me know.

CLEMENT

I will.
He's got to help. (*pointing to Ruby*)

POP

He will.

RUBY

I'm a quiet person. I'll help by being quiet, like you said.

The sweet cement of peace, you said.
It sounds like death but it's all right.

CLEMENT

Quit babbling.

POP

(*to Ruby*) After all, think of how well we live, how well we eat. It could
be enough.

4. *The Food Trio.*

POP

Rare roast beef,
Liver of calf,
Oyster stew,
Or black mushrooms.

CLEMENT

Imagine yourself full
Of cheese and nuts,
Goat cheese and headcheese
And pomegranates.

RUBY

Yes.
Things like
Chicken soup,
Rice and raisins,
Homemade pie.
And if someone cooked something just for you.

POP

Wild ducks,
Little birds,
Ev'rything tastes good.

CLEMENT

Fruits out of season,
Tomatoes grown in rooms,
All kinds of cherries
To make you merry.
All kinds of berries.

RUBY

My mother could cook, yeh.
She made jam.

She made bread.
And I put it together.
CLEMENT
Wild rice,
Oats, peas, beans, and barley.
Incredible variety.
Nature is berserk.
POP
Fish from salt water,
Lobsters and clams.
You can put your fingers
In forbidden places.
CLEMENT
Crisp little peas
And curly endive,
Pears and melons,
And all the dirty roots.
POP
Sausages,
Hams and chops.
Pigs grow a lot of good meat
But never give it to your children.
ALL
Keep anguish from your door
By eating more and more
For on top of a full stomach
Sits a happy head.
Keep it full.
Keep it full.
Keep it full.
Keep it full.
Keep it full.
Keep it full.

5. *Home. Pop and Draves. Ruby is watching.*

POP
Let me look at you, son.
DRAVES
Look.

POP

You've been causing a commotion in my home. I want it to stop.

DRAVES

Me. Mine.

POP

See? You've been scaring your mother.

DRAVES

She's used to it.

POP

I thought I had a wonderful family. I've been very blind.

DRAVES

I want to get loose from it.

POP

Good. There's been too much screaming around here.

DRAVES

I won't eat your food anymore.

POP

You can eat grass.

DRAVES

No more meat and potatoes. I can live on greener stuff.

POP

Doubtless.

DRAVES

You don't believe me because I don't lie.

POP

You have agreed to lie to me until the times change.
Between what you say and what I hear there are
Noises in my head I can't put my finger on.

DRAVES

What are these noises?

POP

Warnings.
Dreams I am troubled to understand.

DRAVES

Tell me. I have a gift for fortunes.

POP

I will tell you my last dream. If you can explain it, you can take over.
I was an old man. My hair was as white as snow. An angel came to me and
said, "No diversions will be brought to you." Then I was standing in an
open meadow. All at once dead leaves began to fall from the sky, fluttering

130

on me as I ran to meet you. Soon the meadow was covered with them. I was standing up to my knees in them, then up to my neck. My throat began to constrict. The angel rescued me from suffocation only to set the leaves on fire. The flames cupped over the world like a flower. There was no night. We welcomed it. But the leaves came back as eyes — moist, black eyes. They hung in the air. It was more than we could bear. I woke up in sweat and confusion.

DRAVES

I don't believe you. I don't believe in angels saving you. Tell me about dead leaves.

POP

Get out of here.

DRAVES

I'm going.

POP

Go your way to the end and good luck.
Don't let your color change.

6. *Draves's Song. Ruby is watching.*

DRAVES

(*sings*)

> I was dancing down the street
> When some guy grabbed me and said
> "Hey, what lives under the pavement?"
> All I could do was shake my head.
> He said he was Brother Body.
> I had no reason to doubt.
> He looked at me very oddly,
> "Let's dig it up and find out."
>
> I had nothing to lose,
> Nothing to lose, nothing to lose.
> Ev'rything is something.
> Only nothing is nothing.
> And I had nothing to lose.
>
> If you want to get to the center
> You have to break through the crust
> And the helicopter gunners
> Were shooting, kicking up the dust.
> So we started digging like hell

131

And we got down twenty feet.
We heard the earth's iron heart
And then we fell from the heat.

I had nothing to lose,
Nothing to lose, nothing to lose.
Ev'rything is something.
Only nothing is nothing.
And I had nothing to lose.

As soon as we hit the bottom
The jungle started to rise
And the desert and the icebergs
Came out of their disguise.
It started to rumble way down low.
Brother Body spoke so slow.
Sometimes you get what you want
And sometimes you lose what you have.

I had nothing to lose,
Nothing to lose, nothing to lose.
Ev'rything is something.
Only nothing is nothing.
And I had nothing to lose.

7. *Lucy is making a doll out of rags from the rag pile. A primitive, faceless doll.*

LUCY
(*to the audience and the doll*) You displease me. Everything you do is
　　wrong.
And to do it right is very important.
To make it last very difficult.
To make it perfect.
I wish there was some way I could.
Some way I could force.
Some way I could hope to.
I wish I could come closer to the human form.
But I can't let that destroy me.
The thing that would finish you
Is missing in me.
Shit.

Of course, you don't say anything, not Mamma, not anything.
(*sings*)

> All night I hear sirens.
> Ev'ry night the dogs bark.
> I'm helpless to save you
> From the world of the dark.
>
> Fires, bombs, disasters, death, and despair.
>
> The night is behind us.
> The night is inside us.
> I'm undoing myself
> To make you my own.
>
> Fires, bombs, disasters, death, and despair.
>
> I'll search below dunghills
> To find the spare sweetness
> The world has to offer.
> I hope you can bless.
>
> Fires, bombs, disasters, death, and despair.
>
> But it won't be enough.
> You'll want to search farther.
> You'll want to fuck stars
> And all you can see.
>
> Fires, bombs, disasters, death, and despair.

8. *Home. Pop asks mutely for the doll, but Lucy refuses to give it.*

POP
You displease me.
Everything you do is wrong.
LUCY
It's true.
POP
Look at that skinny thing. What's the sense?
No sense. You're too old for dolls.
LUCY
I'm done with this one.
POP
It's limp.

LUCY
Can't stand up.
POP
Insane flopping.
LUCY
The face is dull.
It has no life of its own.
POP
It'll be in the way.
I'll want to sit down
And there it will be.

9. *Home. Mom and Draves.*

DRAVES
Why is it so dark in here?
MOM
The days are short this time of year.
DRAVES
Can you still welcome me?
MOM
You keep coming back; yes, I can still welcome you.
DRAVES
I seem to be coming and going a lot lately.
MOM
Come and sit here by me.
Do you have a girl now?
DRAVES
Yes.
MOM
My dearest wish is that you will marry and have a family of your own.
Then you will truly come back to us.
DRAVES
All that ugliness started over again with me. I couldn't.
MOM
When I was pregnant with you, I too wanted only beautiful things. I tried
to keep all ugliness from me for your sake.
DRAVES
It didn't matter to me. I was inside.
MOM
I knew that.

And when you were a little boy, you would always reach your arms out to me. I could never resist.

DRAVES

Why do you keep telling me these things over and over?

MOM

The more I try to show you I love you, the more I am clumsy and fall back upon the past.

DRAVES

Sitting in the past, waiting, you search for reasons to keep me here.

MOM

I thought my love was strong enough to encompass all of you in peace — here at least there would be peace.

DRAVES

Impossible.

MOM

When I listen to you, tears run down my face and I don't even know it.

DRAVES

Between his hate and your love, there is no peace for me here.

10. *Theresa's room. Ruby is watching.*

DRAVES

Let's just go out into the garden.

THERESA

If we can keep walking.

DRAVES

Always thrashing about.
I could make you calm.

THERESA

It's not what I want.
You couldn't.

DRAVES

What do you want? Do you know that anymore?

THERESA

A baby.

DRAVES

You're crazy.

THERESA

I am.

DRAVES

You wouldn't trick me into that, would you?

THERESA

I don't think you're the right man.

DRAVES

Another child for the world. A last mouth for the last morsel. What does it matter who its father is?

THERESA

It matters. It must be a pleasure to plant a child knowingly. It must make you feel competent. It must make you feel like a man.

DRAVES

Not when you think of its future. I like my pleasures unconnected to the future.

THERESA

Your body doesn't get enough of your love. That's the proof of it.

DRAVES

That must be a woman's thing. You can love it.

THERESA

Not enough. You could love every muscle.

DRAVES

The mind's a muscle too, expanding and contracting. I can bring myself to love that.

THERESA

There used to be the whole man, the whole world.

DRAVES

I don't care.

Show me your whole self.

THERESA

Naked you mean?

DRAVES

No. You know what I mean. Show me something of yourself.

I haven't seen anything for a long time.

You haven't been looking at me either.

THERESA

No.

DRAVES

Look at me, right in the eye.

THERESA

No, I'm not up to that.

I'll look at that. (*points to cock, even touches it*)

Where has it been? Show me that.

In what caves and pits never known to me?

DRAVES

I wasn't born for you only.

THERESA

How do you know? I choose all my lovers with you in mind.
Which man will make me smell good to you?

DRAVES

You smell good. (*They embrace.*)

I hate this fucking ritual. (*All the other characters come around to watch them make love. Dissolve to Scene 11.*)

11. *The Family Reunion. Three scenes take place at once, the characters in the first two scenes turn to watch the third when it becomes more intense than their own scene.*

i. *Theresa, Draves, and Clement.*

DRAVES

I used to live here.

CLEMENT

Sure we all did.

THERESA

It's not a bad place.

DRAVES

It's very thick here. I was suffocating.

CLEMENT

Sure.

DRAVES

The food was good but I couldn't eat it.

THERESA

It's the normal thing. You're no different from the rest of us.

CLEMENT

Right. We all think we're so smart.

DRAVES

Do we? Are we?

CLEMENT

It doesn't make any difference one way or the other.

THERESA

It's just another thing to get over.

ii. *Mom and Lucy.*

MOM

Look how the light has changed since I last looked out.

LUCY

It's much darker. You ought to look out more often. Then the changes wouldn't scare you.

MOM

You look out for me.

LUCY

Oh, mother.

MOM

I have a headache.

LUCY

Right there on your head? Pain?

MOM

A headache.

LUCY

All of this on your mind? On your head?

MOM

All of what?

LUCY

Oh, mother.

MOM

You think you're so smart. I wish you were.

LUCY

Oh, mother.

iii. *Pop and Ruby.*

POP

Think of a pattern from anyplace.
One that pleases you.
And if you can't think of one
Let me show you mine.

RUBY

Show me yours.

POP

I want you to try to think of one first.

RUBY

What if I don't believe in patterns?

POP

The more fool you.

RUBY

Did we both come from the same mother?

POP

Hardly. What does that mean?

RUBY

I asked first.

POP

For God's sake, find a point of view for your life.

RUBY

I have a point of view. Yours has got to have more life to it.

POP

What my life needs is more point.

RUBY

More life.

Here — let's touch tongues.

That's life. Simple and sure.

POP

No. I don't want to touch you like that. That just confuses things. That is ugly to me.

RUBY

Then you need to touch the most. (*offers tongue again*)

POP

No, I won't! You've lost your wits.

RUBY

Losing and gaining, losing and gaining. That's life. Here. (*offers tongue again*)

POP

Get back. Get away. Get back over there.

You're dying faster than the rest of us.

RUBY

Please.

POP

(*knocks Ruby down, speaks to the others*) I won't kill him.

I'll follow him everywhere

And take away his secrets.

PART TWO

1. *Clement and Draves come in through the audience.*

DRAVES

This city stinks.

CLEMENT

Yes.

DRAVES

Nothing but garbage.

CLEMENT

There's safety in garbage, don't you feel it?

DRAVES

Shit. Children popping out all over.

CLEMENT

A giant hand squeezes them out of places you've never dreamt of.

DRAVES

Same old hole.

CLEMENT

Fuck it and be happy.

DRAVES

I have and I'm not.

2. *Theresa's room. Theresa and Draves, Ruby watching from a way off. Clement brings Pop to a place where he can watch secretly.*

THERESA

(*sings*)

> Come with me slowly.
> Lay down your knife.
> The man in the window
> Is only your life.
>
> Lift up your stone head.
> Leave me behind.
> Men's mouths will rob you
> Of the need to be kind.
>
> Then I'll take you back.
> Naked, divine,
> And peeling your secrets
> I'll make you mine.

(*Clement enters.*)

DRAVES

Good. You're back.

CLEMENT

Have you been waiting? Are you ready?

DRAVES
Yes.

CLEMENT
Are you ready? I'm going to extract a little spinal fluid from her and inject it into you. Are you ready for that?

DRAVES
Yes.

CLEMENT
(*to Theresa*) Do you accept all these dangers so lightly?

THERESA
Yes, it's all right.

CLEMENT
Shall I tell you again about the Brothers of the Left Hand and the meaning of this ritual?

DRAVES
We don't want to hear that mystical crap. Just do it.

CLEMENT
I wanted to be sure. I never would have believed you'd go this far.

DRAVES
Is everything clean? Is it sterile?

CLEMENT
Sure. (*to Theresa*) Are you sure now? After we start there's no turning back. And this is it as far as you're concerned. You can't ever do this again.

THERESA
I know.

CLEMENT
Bend over. (*Draves and Theresa bend over, knees straight; Clement extracts fluid from Theresa's spine and injects it into Draves's spine.*)

DRAVES
Does it hurt?

THERESA
Christ yes.

CLEMENT
I have to go right away. I wish I could stay and watch.

THERESA
I wouldn't let you stay and watch. I paid for that privilege myself. I'm not going to share it with you. (*Clement leaves and joins Pop in the secret place.*)

DRAVES

Nothing. Nothing. Nothing.

THERESA

Be patient.

DRAVES

Nothing. Nothing. Nothing.

I don't feel good.

I have a headache. Feel it. My head is very hot.

My eyes are hot too. My head is very light. It's hungry for the blood that belongs in it.

THERESA

Put your head between your knees.

DRAVES

Aaaaaaaaaaaaaah! Help me, you bitch.

THERESA

What is it? What should I do? (*Draves begins to rap. This should be improvised by the actor — a free-associational speech which is careless of both words and ideas, which is flavored with bad and brilliant puns, which takes advantage of all the real attributes of the actress playing Theresa, which takes advantage of the composition of the audience. This rap is interrupted by Theresa at several points. The following dialogue should only be used to suggest the pattern and the style of the speech. Theresa's lines may remain the same.*)

DRAVES

Do. Did I do something? Yes or no. Does anyone do something? I don't know and I don't care. Success. It's so difficult to be a success. I find it so difficult to suck seed. (*laughs*) Suck suck suck. Suck and eat. Just letting the mouth take over, just letting the worlds come out. (*laughs*) Words can kill you but you're never afraid of them. I'll eat my words anyway. I'll have to. (*laughs*) I'll eat them under the covers like cakes. Crumbs all over. Crumbs in the bed. Nothing wordse. Human and cake like. (*laughs*) Night after night voraciously eating cake under the covers. But you can't do it. (*sings*) Do not eat my little cake, for I will kill you if you do. (*laughs*)

THERESA

You have to direct yourself to the question.

DRAVES

What question? What is the question? Shun the quest. That's the answer. It's written in the question. (*laughs*) It's written on the wall. Which side of the wall are you on, sister? There's a question for you. Your brain is a tight wire of questions coming loose. I don't know how you stand it. It's going to jail me. I can feel it. Bars all over. I feel it. Feel it. Oop. You have a crack in your head. Make it stop. Make it stop! I can smell it coming apart. No! I can't look. Oh, that's better. You've covered it up with your hair.

THERESA

It's no good. You've got to concentrate.

DRAVES

It's no good. What is? (*shouts*) What is? Concentrate. Put things together. One and one and me and you. Hung up on one and one. Poor girl. You make a gesture of granting favors, but you're hung up on one and one. Poor girl. I hope next time you've gone past that. Two and two. I think you could try for that without injury. Injury. Injury. The light in here is coming so slowly down in shafts. They're going to do me an injury. Look at that one over there. So evil. Evil devil (*laughs*) We all know that.

THERESA

You're wasting time. There isn't much time left. You're wasting it. Quit moving around. Keep your body still.

DRAVES

What is to be done with the wastes? Put in plastic bags and floated into space. That's what it's for out there. A wasteland for wastes. That's what this is too.

THERESA

Please do it right for my sake.

DRAVES

Your sake? You know what's yours, besides your sake? The stuff that runs from your nose to your mouth. That's what's yours. My father used to say that. Think of all the body fluids all over everything. Everything is all slimy with them, we slip around all over on them. Slip, slip — a mere slip of a slip. (*laughs*) Receptacles for fluids stand all about. But the body tricks you, sends them up when you're not near a receptacle. No control over them at all. Sometimes worse than others.

THERESA

None of my guts have gone into you.

DRAVES

Oh, yes, they have, baby. Listen, they're making me jump. Listen, you bitch. Not just your guts, no — you weren't content with that — no, no — your hatred too, your self-hate and your hate of me. Your lust for a baby, all those things I can't stand about you have gone into me. Just like my mother. She injected me at birth — but you waited till I had more weapons — you knew you could still injure — you knew, you bitch. Anxious, now

143

I'm anxious with your anxiety without knowing what it's all about. Without knowing. But I know what you're about. You're right here with me under my skin now, itching. And I hate it. I hate you. I see you as you really are. And I don't even like you anymore. Go away from me, as far as you can. (*Shakes her*) Go on, go on, find some other sucker to play with. Your arms are just growing and growing — you're trying to suck me into you but instead I've sucked you into me — Christ! (*hits her*) Go away! (*Theresa goes away. Draves watches her go, getting more and more agitated, babbling now. Words extended as far as possible, gibberish, screams, till he falls down silent. Pop and Clement come down from their secret place and stand by looking at him for a while and after Theresa.*)

POP
(*sings*)

> The snatch of the sea is naked now.
> Everyone is dancing alone away.
> The walls are down within and out
> But the kingdom of heaven is lost.
>
> Pushing upward in darkness we've come
> Like birds with tar on our wings
> Flapping wildly, singing of flight,
> Wild to feel someone listening.
>
> And love is invisible anyway
> Out of sight in the sea-wrack
> But felt falling close to the water
> Or floating in the fearful fog.

3. *The Search.*

RUBY

(*goes over to Draves who is still lying on the floor and touches him and speaks*) I was lying on the grass, obeying . . (*Ruby is pushed away from Draves by Pop and taken to a central place where his clothes and body are meticulously examined, and he is naked. When they're through, they tap him gently and he falls down, circling round and round on his hands and knees. During this scene Draves has dragged himself over to Lucy's rag pile and he is made into a doll by Lucy. Ruby and Draves watch each other all during the scene. After Pop and Clement have left, Ruby goes to the audience.*) Excuse me, do you have something I can put on? (*When he is given something he puts it on.*) Thank you, nothing will happen to it.

4. *Ruby reenters from the audience. Lucy is still dressing Draves in rags. Ruby makes a sound and gesture of request, no word.*

DRAVES

Why do you keep following me?

RUBY

I thought you were following me.

DRAVES

No.

RUBY

There you are every time I turn around.

DRAVES

How many times do you turn around?

RUBY

(*shrugs*) I was stopped last night, but I'm all right.

DRAVES

You look all right.

LUCY

I hope you're all right.

RUBY

I said I was. I adopted the position with arms over head, crouched down. The civil position.

DRAVES

The civil rights position?

RUBY

That's it. They couldn't get at me.

DRAVES

So what? (*Ruby starts to rip all the rags off Draves. Lucy hits him with the rags and chases him.*) Why do you keep asking for it?

RUBY

If someone in the world is being hit, why not me?

DRAVES

A hell of an attitude.

RUBY

I've always hoped to get something back. Here, I want to give you this. (*offers the garment the audience has given him*)

DRAVES

No, you can't trick me so easily. I won't take it.

RUBY

Next time.

CLEMENT
(*with Pop at the other side of the stage*) Look at that poor bastard.
(*laughs*)

5. *The Questioning. Clement's laugh extends to all the characters and, it is hoped, the audience. Ruby is suddenly in center stage with one spotlight on him and all other lights out. The light comes from directly above.*

POP
Tell me about yourself. Something I don't know.

RUBY
Sure. I'm a white male, blond hair, blue eyes, a tattoo on the upper right thigh which says "Mother, I'm Coming Home." No noticeable scars.

POP
I know that. That's not what I had in mind.

RUBY
What do you have in mind for me?

POP
I'll ask the questions.

MOM
Are you warm enough?

RUBY
Oh, yes, thank you.

LUCY
Show us your tongue. (*Ruby shows her.*) Thank you, it's lovely.

MOM
I've seen it before.
Were you happy at home?

RUBY
Yes.

MOM
Did you love your mother?

RUBY
Yes, she was a lovely person.
She used to take baths with me,
Warm water, leaning next to her,
Big towels rubbing.
I'll never forget.

LUCY
Have you loved women?

RUBY
Yes.

LUCY
Have you loved men?

RUBY
Yes.

LUCY
Which sex do you prefer?

RUBY
I don't prefer.

MOM
You don't have to answer everything.
You can say you don't know.
You can say you don't remember.

RUBY
I don't know.
I don't remember.

DRAVES
How do you feel about freedom?

RUBY
Freedom, yes.
Freedom to float without touching anything but the water,
Freedom to fall . .

POP
Come to the point.

RUBY
Never saw the point,
Never saw the road,
Never nothing.

POP
You piss me off.
You know what I think?
I think you're keeping things from us.

RUBY
I don't have any things to keep.

LUCY
Do you plan ahead of time?

RUBY
A head of time?

DRAVES

Why are you always watching me?

RUBY

Because I think I know you.

THERESA

Why do men want to know other men?

RUBY

They think it's the only thing.

THERESA

Is it?

CLEMENT

Are you more miserable than most people?

RUBY

I don't know.

CLEMENT

Take a guess.

RUBY

I don't know.

CLEMENT

You can guess about anything. **Guess.**

RUBY

Yes.

CLEMENT

Do you feel I like you?

RUBY

Guess.

MOM

Are you lonely for your mother?
Were you sorry when she died?

RUBY

She isn't dead.

MOM

I'm sorry.

LUCY

When were you born?

RUBY

When I knew it was impossible.

POP

When you knew what was impossible? **Being** born? Why are you playing with us?

DRAVES
Are you trying to be a martyr?
RUBY
I'm not a martyr you can call your own.
DRAVES
But do you express your opinion?
RUBY
I've always talked too much.
DRAVES
Have people told you that?
RUBY
No. I have just felt that I have talked when I should not have talked.
MOM
But you must talk.
That's why you're here.
So we can listen.
POP
Are you happy with what you've made of yourself?
RUBY
A man who is not good or wise or beautiful is perfectly happy with himself.
POP
What does that mean? Is that you? Not good or wise or beautiful? Why do you keep avoiding the questions? Why do you avoid answering?
RUBY
I'm sorry. I'll try.
I will answer.
POP
Did you know that most of the world is crying?
RUBY
Yes, I knew that. I wanted . .
POP
Did you know that people everywhere are crying?
RUBY
Yes, I wanted . .
POP
Why have you made everyone cry? (*Silence. Then all the actors together ask, "Why have you made everyone cry?" Then the questions from before are asked again randomly, not waiting for answers, getting louder, harsher, till Ruby breaks down.*)

149

RUBY

So many of you . . so many of them . . condemned me to die by water drops. I've tried to die. I really have tried. I bit myself making my arms and legs bleed, biting especially the veins and vulnerable parts. I rolled myself up in rugs. I strangled my balls. I did it. I admit it. I only did it for the people I love. And then I saw you were killing my family in front of me with lightbulbs, garbage cans, with double-edged blades, crushing them with sounds they couldn't understand, shoving their eyes in the dust as if they were dust. You even decapitated them with razor blades after burying them up to their very necks in the soft dirt. Yes, and even the children. And the blade wasn't even sharp, wasn't meant to be, but was pushed by that bull machine to knock over heads. And afterwards a field of speechless stumps. I can still hear the screaming. Those screams are inside my head separately from me now. I can't die because I have to scream. Someone had to do it. Me. I said I would do it. I said I would do it. I've brought shame down on my family. My people they won't survive it. Some of them are being kept alive to make me talk. But I won't tell. I haven't told you anything.

They've given me pills to make me smell like shit. People won't come near me anymore.

POP

He's raving.

LUCY

Take him to his rest. Strangled his balls, how?

RUBY

I'm not through. I'll never be done. I want you to hear everything.

No, I've been vulgar. I've offended you. My smell has hurt you. I'll go now. (*Ruby leaves through the audience, saying*, "I'm sorry. Excuse me. I'm sorry I have offended you. I've made a mistake. I only . ." *He re-enters from the back of the house.*) This is called the Fool's Song. (*sings*)

> Shall I live in a treeless jungle?
> Shall there be no more green alive?
> Shall I live in dust with no water?
> Shall I be the only wild thing left
>
> After the great convulsion
> Shakes the earth,
> Shakes the earth,
> Shakes the earth?
>
> Will I live in dust with no water to make mud?

They've set fire to the green sea
And poisoned the innocent ground.
They're giving cancer to the sweet plants.
Shall I be the only wild thing left?

No more avalanche lilies
On high mountain meadows.
No more sunfish, prairie dogs
         great cats, eagles.
No more sweet animals but me.
Will I be alone in the world?
Will I be alone in the world?

(*leaves*)
   CLEMENT
(*sings*)

People should be dead
They'd be better off
Though they don't know it
And lust after children.

People should be dead
Before they die anyway.
Before the sun goes down
And the sea goes in.

We don't belong here.
No, none of us do.
We'll leave in darkness
When the world falls dead.

6. *Two scenes in different areas in the theatre. In one, Pop and Lucy are talking very quietly, in the other, Theresa and Ruby. Theresa is dressing Ruby. They do not happen together but are intercut.*

   THERESA
I appreciate your suffering and all that.
But it's so selfish just to stand there and suffer.
Don't you have any guts?
   RUBY
I have no answer to that.
   THERESA
Wouldn't it please you to do one impossible thing?
One impossible thing and then die quickly?

RUBY

Maybe. Yes. If it was the right thing.

THERESA

The right thing. How would you know for sure?

POP

(*to Lucy*) I think my heart is stopping.

LUCY

You can't just sit there,

Listening to your heart tick.

POP

I'm almost an old man, I don't even have a garden to tend in my old age. Things in rows were always a temptation to me.

LUCY

People in rows.

POP

The world was vivid then. Never since. Never since. It was because I was alone. I could see better then. People have always muddied things up for me.

LUCY

There are too many people.

POP

I hoped for something quite modest. A little awakening. And instead this madness. I'm going to leave it.

THERESA

(*to Ruby*) I'm going to kill him, that man who dreams of old orders. I want to set changes loose in the world. It changes so slowly.

RUBY

He's only one man. It's thousands of years past killing one man.

THERESA

I think that's right. I am only one. But I have to take my anger and look him in the face with it. We don't even know where our bread comes from anymore. That kind of knowledge has been denied us and for what? It's no use pretending that because you're the victim you're better than they are. We are none of us civilized. Not one. We are not innocent. Why keep it a secret?

RUBY

I'll go with you, but I won't do it.

THERESA

If you go with me, you'll do it.

It takes madness, remember that. It takes madness to deal with power

so absurd. Killing's not so hard. I can do it. I can go that far. See this?
(*brings out a gun*)

RUBY

Put it away.

THERESA

Put your hand on it first.

RUBY

(*touches it*) It's cold.

THERESA

You better believe it.

POP

Where is my Lucy? (*Ruby and Theresa enter Pop's room. They are falling all over each other, a comic but lethal duo.*) You're not my Lucy.

THERESA

(*fumbling with her gun*) I'm going to kill you.

POP

Kill me? (*Stands up in alarm; Theresa drops the gun.*)

RUBY

Give it to me.

POP

You too? Kill me?
I never meant you any harm.

THERESA

(*grabs the gun*) Give it to me.
You'll never be able to do it. (*She pulls the trigger but the gun does not go off.*)

POP

Lucy! Where are you? (*All three tussle for the gun. It falls and is kicked. It goes off and kills Pop.*)

THERESA

It was kind of an accident. We both did it. (*Ruby goes over to Pop and listens to his heart, putting his head on Pop's chest, embracing him.*) Is he dead?

RUBY

A few rumblings.

THERESA

Or dying. We've got to get out of here. (*Ruby and Theresa make a noisy and clumsy exit, Theresa dragging Ruby out of there. Lucy comes to the body and mourns over it, speaking to the body, to Ruby and Theresa, to the audience.*)

LUCY

Don't talk. Don't move.
Why couldn't I be mute?
And deaf and blind?
Don't talk, don't move.
Don't talk, don't move.
Don't talk, don't move.

7. *Mom comes down to where Lucy and Pop are lying still on the floor.*

MOM

It's sort of awful, looking in the mirror and
Seeing all the scars. It's scary. I close my eyes
Because we have only one body.
The scars really are very beautiful. They're pretty
In a funny way. They're like a dress. They're like
A tribal mark. They are my own.
It's just that they remind me that I'm still sick,
And I don't know if I'll ever be well.

8. *The Funeral. Ruby, Clement, Mom, and Theresa put Pop's body on a high table or on a slanted board against the wall. They light incense and pass it to the audience. Mom, Lucy, and Clement dress the body in rags from Lucy's rag pile, very slowly, in a ritual way, making Pop's body a totem. Draves beats the drum as for a fallen chief of state. It takes a long time.*

LUCY

(*sings*)

In the name of all the people in the world who have not
reached heaven and will not. They must go underground
with you. You were the only one of their deceivers.
In the name of all the people who have no way. In the
name of all the people who will not reach heaven.

O father
I didn't know you
Would die in front of me.
O father
I didn't know
I would have to watch.
O father

I didn't know
I would be spared by silence.

I let you slip away without a word.
Then the words choked me
Blundering out too late.

O father
I saw your pain
But I wouldn't touch it.
O father
I never knew you
Would die in front of me.

DRAVES

(*beats on the drum and shouts*) It's not him. That's not my father.
Look at him, dressed like a king.
Dressed like Lucy's doll.
Look at the poor bastard. (*picks up the body and throws it over his shoulder; the others try to stop him*)
Do you think I'll break his stiff body? Look at him!
A shell!

LUCY

Take him down, take him down.

DRAVES

(*pushes his mother away, takes away the rags she is holding*) Stay back now. Stay back. Don't come close or I'll bite him, I'll chew him to shreds. I'll desecrate him the way he deserves. Take your eyes away from this dead thing. There's nothing there. (*throws Pop's body in a corner*) Look at this arm, this strong right hand. It's been a lot of places but it's only got one more to go, crossed neatly over the heart. The heart is not redeemable either; the same blood has washed around it for twenty years; the arteries are clogged with waste. For he lived a life of reasonable caution. He didn't take chances with his arm or his heart.

I prefer to take chances, I prefer excess. It's a way of killing yourself. Then no one has to do it for you.

(*to Mom*) Don't pity him. Don't think of him as the victim. For I want you to know he would have taken everyone with him. He was so afraid of dying that he would have taken everyone. Now we're going to throw him down in the pit and bring the earth down on him. (*throws rags on him*) And then we're going to be glad.

The dead know nothing.
All that dark is blinding.
Let us turn to the light
The impure messenger of the sun, of the sun, of the sun.
Let us turn to the sun. (*Sings, over and over, the others joining with their own songs, till all are singing or chanting together but each singing his own song; they come together bodily as well.*)

> Let us turn to the sun.
> Let us turn to the sun.
> Let us turn to the sun.

RUBY

> I'm afraid of the dark.
> I'm afraid of the dark.

MOM

> Morning quiets my fear.
> Morning quiets my fear.

LUCY

> The sun is burning.
> Why can't I be burning?
> The sun is burning.
> Why can't I be burning?

CLEMENT

> Even if the sun is sour.
> Even if your eyes burst
> Staring straight at the sun
> Staring straight at the sun.

(*Now all but Theresa are hanging onto one another under a single light, looking at the light, each singing his own song. Theresa bangs on her tambourine and they stop and listen.*)

THERESA

What good is its turning?
What good is its burning?
What good is this hard life?
Even I can kill it.
(*sings*)

> Let us burn on earth.
> Let us be our own sun.
> Let us burn on earth.
> Let us be our own sun.

(*Everyone starts again with his own thing. But one by one they struggle to leave the group and join Theresa, singing and dancing her melody. When Draves is all alone singing* "Let us turn to the sun," *the light goes out.*)

PART THREE

The cave. The light is very special. It comes from above in drops which illumine only the specific area underneath. There are no shadows but much darkness.

POP

(*reincarnated as the cave dweller*) Welcome to Mother Earth. You've asked for her and here you are. She's old here. This cave is millions of years old, older than the first man or even the first thing that resembled you. All the evidence points to its long life. In this room the walls drip. Things fall from the walls and cause confusion. And here invisible wars are raging all the time. You must let the dirt fall on your head. That is the essence of this place. For a cave is an essential place, out of the sky, under the ground, under the dirt. You've wanted such a place nearly since you've been born. I don't know what lives in here with us. Some creatures do, nature is persistent.

This room is connected to other rooms by narrow tunnels. I cannot speak for them. You can only reach them on your hands and knees. You'll want to stay in this room. For in here the reverberations can be finely tuned, tuned even as far as music. Perhaps you will learn to do it.

DRAVES

How can I live in this inhuman darkness?

POP

Darkness is human.

DRAVES

I should have stayed in the light.

POP

You couldn't.

DRAVES

If I listen to your back and forth, I'll lose my way.

POP

There isn't any way of your own; there is only the way.

DRAVES

Who are you, even now, to order my life, to make structures for me which I only need to fill in. Who are you to require such things of me?

157

POP

Your father. Fathers have rights by reason of the gifts we have given you.

DRAVES

I want to give them back.

POP

It's too late. You've made them your own.

DRAVES

I want to give back whatever I can. (*takes off his clothes down to, say, a jock strap, and lays them in front of his father*) This one cloth I will keep so as not to be humbled in front of you.

POP

This return of goods is unnecessary. You'll only come under the power of other fathers.

DRAVES

There will be no other fathers in my life.

POP

Take nothing for your journey then.

DRAVES

I'm cold, cold, cold. I've been cold for years without feeling it. I need someone to kiss me, I need someone to hold me. I need someone to kiss my hands. Who will do it? It can't be a father. (*goes into audience*) Will you do it? Will you do it?
No, I can see you won't. I'm sorry I've made a mistake. (*Draves freezes into a rigid block.*)

CLEMENT

Frozen. That last humiliation did it.

RUBY

He'll come around. (*The actors warm Draves's body, blowing on it and kissing it.*) Sh sh sh.

DRAVES

I came late.

RUBY

A place has been saved for you.

DRAVES

I didn't know it was possible.

RUBY

Yes. She did it. That woman over there.

DRAVES

She has blood in her eyes.

RUBY

That's not blood. It's a welcome to you.

DRAVES

Is she mine?

CLEMENT

Mine, mine. Aren't you past that? Haven't you grown up yet? How could she be yours at this distance?

DRAVES

She wants me.

RUBY

Come and see.

MOM

Will you kiss my mouth? Some dirt from the cave fell on my mouth and now my mouth is diseased. My lips are full of pus. Will you kiss them? They're bleeding. Will you cool them? They came to be sore because of the dirt. The dirt from the cave which I could not get out. I clawed at my mouth until it was sore. There is still dirt. Will you kiss it away?

DRAVES

Will I too be diseased?

MOM

Yes or no.

DRAVES

It's a trap. It's a trap if I kiss your mouth.

MOM

If I kiss your mouth. (*Mom kisses him on the mouth.*)

THERESA

Kiss me too.

DRAVES

You're someone else. There isn't a reason.

THERESA

Words are reasons. You're never at a loss for words, you know. Come and lie down with me.

DRAVES

Let's lie down here in the dark.

THERESA

No, come over here in the light.

DRAVES

But that's a fire.

THERESA

No, you're mistaken.

If it's a fire, I'll protect you from it.

DRAVES

But the flames. Even if I lie on you, how can I embrace you, how can I enjoy you?

THERESA

Try it and see. There are no flames. (*They lie down; Theresa lies comfortably but Draves burns.*)

DRAVES

(*gets up with a shriek*) I'm burning. You lied to me.

THERESA

I knew you wouldn't stay.

CLEMENT

(*comes and drags Draves away, tying his legs together with a rope*) Are you coming down with me?

DRAVES

Down where?

CLEMENT

Down. (*drags him to the audience*)

DRAVES

I'm a nigger.

My skin has turned black through the years, blacker and blacker through the years. At first I tried to stop it. But soon I realized that it was inevitable. Now I am untouchable. Touch me.

CLEMENT

(*hits him very hard on his bare back*) You let your color change. It was an injunction on you at birth not to let your color change. But you did it anyway just to annoy them. It cannot be allowed.

LUCY

(*pulls Draves up from the floor*) Stand there. Get ready. We are going to race. From here to there and here to there and back again. You've got to beat me. The prizes are enormous. You're going to be a rich man. Get ready. Get set. Go. (*Draves falls down, his legs being tied together. Lucy keeps running back and forth.*) Get up. Get up. Get up.

DRAVES

(*to the audience*) Wake up. Wake up.

LUCY

Forget that. Forget them. You haven't got time for that. You've got to make the minimum requirement. (*Draves and Lucy still running. Mom stands in front of Draves.*)

MOM

Once it came to me that my children might hunger for my very body as I have hungered for the bodies of some men. For my very body.

DRAVES

It's not motherly here. Not soft. Not kindly.

LUCY

(*still running*) Oh, you have your motherly vision and I have mine. (*collapses*)

MOM

In a long schooling for being alone, alone like this, my God, I had my children. When I knew that their hunger was for my body I became afraid. Afraid that at the end of the day when their hunger had gone elsewhere, I would perish. (*collapses*)

DRAVES

Lucy, come over here to me.

LUCY

I can't move around too much today.

DRAVES

I'm unable to get there.

LUCY

I have moved around too much today.

CLEMENT

(*to Draves, a sergeant*) Attention. I want this place cleaned up. It smells like creeps in here. It smells like tongues touching. It smells like long hair. Clean it up on the double. (*Clement trips Draves so he lands on the floor and throws a bucket of water on him.*)

DRAVES

(*tries to clean with his body, although his legs are still tied together*) No. It takes more than water. It has to be sweat or saliva or amniotic fluid. Water that the body itself has purified.

RUBY

(*untying Draves, calming him*) I was lying on the grass, obeying. I was in a high mountain meadow. Because of the sky. It was a land independent of a man's walking on it. Or so it seemed to me. I was waiting for something to come and move me. There were incredible flowers. The girl knew them all by name. But I didn't care about their names or even hers. What amazed me was the tenaciousness of those flowers in that tough place.

Their fragility and diversity. Nature had found so many answers to the same condition of earth, water, air, and sun that I felt bereft. Nothing could comfort me.

The blossoms were small, little bells and stars. Their perfect forms took my breath away. I could only wonder why there were so many answers. And against those flowers my manliness has no defense. In my life then I came to see that other things were like those flowers — fish, grass, grains, people.

But I forgot. I forgot it over and over. At the crucial moment I always forgot. (*Draves washes his face and body with the water on the floor. From their stiff positions the actors begin to sing their part of the sun song. Draves goes to each of the actors with water or just himself and they begin to dance. Pop has taken over Draves's line* "Let us turn to the sun." *Draves adds a new line to the song, on top of all the others:* "The sun has taken our sleep." *They all dance and sing their own song to exhaustion.*)

Rags by Nancy Walter opened on December 15, 1969, at the Firehouse Theatre, Minneapolis, Minnesota. It was directed by Sydney S. Walter.

Cast of Characters

POP	Paul Boesing
MOM	Muniera Jakobi
DRAVES	Bill Lampe
LUCY	Antoinette Maher
RUBY	Marlow Hotchkiss
THERESA	Carol Swardson
CLEMENT	Mark Donicht

STEPHEN GRECCO

The Orientals

The Setting

A small third-floor efficiency in an old city brownstone. The back wall has two windows which look down upon the street. Between them a marble fireplace containing a makeshift bookcase instead of the customary andirons. Above the mantel a large oriental print; on the mantel, partially hidden by a stack of books, a pair of black opera glasses. In the room a large brass bed upper right, an easy chair and reading lamp down right, an overstuffed sofa down left, a bureau and a cage with a myna bird upper left. The apartment door, left, leads to a narrow hallway which can be seen. Exit right goes to an offstage kitchenette and bathroom. The room is clean and well ordered.

THE ORIENTALS

Late March. Early evening. At rise, Michael appears in the hallway. He is 30, of average looks and height. He wears a navy blue raincoat and a large burgundy scarf — both wringing wet. He pauses in front of the door and lays two small packages on the floor as he searches for his key. He finds it and enters. On a nearby coatrack he carefully hangs his wraps, then returns to the hallway for the packages, which he puts on an end table next to the easy chair. He closes the door and hums quietly. He walks upstage, stands, looks about the room; he sees the opera glasses, picks them up, and peers out of the window on the left. He mumbles something to himself, puts the glasses back, goes into the kitchenette offstage. Sound of running water. He comes out holding a wine glass and a corkscrew, goes to the easy chair, and takes a bottle of claret from one of the packages. He opens it, pours, removes a book from the other bag, and turns on the lamp. He sips the wine and begins to read. Slow fade to blackout. Fade up on room. Michael has fallen asleep in the chair; the book is in his lap. It is dark outside; the only light in the room comes from the floorlamp and from the streetlight shining through the windows. Suddenly a man appears in the hallway. He is about 45, heavyset, and expensively dressed. He pauses in front of the door for a moment, then knocks. Michael is half asleep when he answers.

MICHAEL
Yes?

MAN
Pardon me, do you happen to have the correct time?

MICHAEL

What? Oh . . uh . . (*Michael absently looks at his bare wrist, then goes to the bureau to check the clock. The man enters the room and looks around.*) It's ten forty-five. (*slight pause*) I said it's . . ten forty-five.

MAN

Ten forty-five, you say? Hmmm. (*He checks his watch.*) Mine says ten forty-five also. (*cheerfully*) Either we're both right — or both wrong. (*Slight pause. Michael begins walking toward the door.*) It's a pity, but I can never be certain of the time anymore. I dropped my watch one night at the opera— *The Magic Flute*, I believe — and it's been worrying me ever since. Rather expensive, too. Swiss, forty-three jewels. I bought it last summer in Ankara. Wonderful place, Ankara. Have you ever been to Turkey?

MICHAEL

(*at door*) Uh . . no. You'll have to excuse me.

MAN

Yes, of course. Thanks ever so much. (*He starts to walk out, but stops as he reaches the door.*) You're Michael McVey, aren't you?

MICHAEL

That's right. Who are you?

MAN

My name is Farber — Elliott Farber. You don't know me, however. At least I don't think you do. I suppose you're wondering how I know your name. Well, I'll be very obliging and tell you. But first I'd like to sit down.

MICHAEL

I'm sorry (*begins to close door*), but I have some reading to do.

ELLIOTT

Please don't be alarmed. I can assure you I'm not one of those crazed degenerates that roam our lovely city. I'm as wary of strangers as you are. I'll only be a moment. (*Michael closes door.*)

MICHAEL

Do you have something to tell me?

ELLIOTT

(*pleasantly*) No. I have something to ask you. (*pause*)

MICHAEL

Go on.

ELLIOTT

It's awkward for me to say. As you may have already guessed, I really wasn't looking for the time when I knocked at your door. I was going to ask you, right then and there, but I found it . . difficult to say the words.

Nevertheless, I won't hold you up — ha, ha — *take* any more of your time.
So I'll get right to the point. (*slight pause*) Do you know Helene Carlyle?

MICHAEL

Helene . . Carlyle. No, I've never heard of her.

ELLIOTT

Please be honest with me. I must know.

MICHAEL

I already told you. I don't know who she is. (*slight pause*)

ELLIOTT

She claims to know you.

MICHAEL

Does she?

ELLIOTT

She claims to know you . . very well.

MICHAEL

(*impatiently*) Whoever she is, she's lying.

ELLIOTT

(*not affronted*) Helene is my fiancée. To my knowledge, she has never
lied to me.

MICHAEL

Then she obviously has me confused with someone else.

ELLIOTT

That, sir, is unlikely. Too many things fit in. (*walking around the room*)
The oriental print, the bookcase, the myna bird, the . . brass bed.

MICHAEL

What are you trying to say?

ELLIOTT

(*coolly, dryly*) I'm . . saying that you've been seeing Helene — my
fiancée.

MICHAEL

I think you'd better leave.

ELLIOTT

Oh, now, don't misunderstand me. I've not come here to chastise you.
What Helene does before we're married is of little concern to me. I simply
want to make it very clear that I will not allow this type of activity after
we've exchanged our marital vows. We're to be married soon.

MICHAEL

Congratulations. Now fluff off.

ELLIOTT

As you wish. (*walks toward door; stops*) Mr. McVey, I'm not the kind of person who likes to relate unwholesome details, but as you well know by now, Helene suffers from a . . slight emotional disturbance. I've known it for some time and have done my best to help her. We all have. Mother looks upon Helene as her own daughter. Father thinks the world of her. Even my brother, Goodwin, calls her Sis. She's like one of the family, really. It is our hope that one day she will in fact be. You understand my concern.

MICHAEL

Yes, I do. But . .

ELLIOTT

(*interrupting*) Helene has a lot in her favor— youth, good looks, loads of talent. A born musician, without a doubt. Loves to play the clavichord. That's how I met her — at a clavichord recital. She used to play the French horn, but she doesn't anymore.

MICHAEL

It breaks me up to hear that. Now, look, I've told you twice — this Helene, for me, is an unknown quantity.

ELLIOTT

There's no need to spare feelings. You're not the first one, you know. There have been others. What's done is done. However . .

MICHAEL

(*grabbing Elliott*) Nothing has been done — not by me, anyway. Now it's getting past your bedtime.

ELLIOTT

(*freeing himself*) Nothing? I wonder if you could tell that to me in front of Helene. Could you keep a straight face. I doubt it. No, you would probably snicker and wink . . and maybe even chuckle. Oh, you're a clever one, Mr. McVey. I know your type. You have a very clever way of . . interfering with people.

MICHAEL

Get out . .

ELLIOTT

Not until I've finished.

MICHAEL

You're finished right now!

ELLIOTT

(*walking around room*) Yes, she told me about it. How you sensed her . . her weakness, and how you took advantage of it. It was in January, wasn't it? At Jason's. You were in men's furnishings; she was there, too — shopping for a gift. For me, in case you were wondering. (*Elliott picks up the*

168

opera glasses, then puts them back.) You watched her for a time — "sized her up" to be more precise — and then followed her to the counter displaying men's briefs. You said: "The briefs are very brief, aren't they?" She said: "What?" You said, "I said the briefs are very brief, aren't they?" She said: "Are they?" You said: "Look for yourself." She looked and smiled. You said: "That's how they're making them this year." She said: "How did they make them last year?" (*slight pause*) It isn't necessary for me to continue. (*slight pause*) I . . I feel somewhat faint; may I trouble you for a glass of water? (*Michael goes into the kitchenette. Elliott sits in the easy chair and removes his gloves. Michael returns with the water.*) Thank you. These scenes are terribly upsetting for me. I thought by now I'd have been used to them. (*He drinks, puts the glass on the end table, and picks up the book that Michael had been reading.*) So you've been doing some reading. I think reading is wonderful, but unfortunately I don't get much of a chance to read for pleasure anymore. Father is getting up in years and most of the responsibilities of the estate are falling onto my shoulders. Not that I'm complaining. By the way, have you ever read *The Siege of Fuku* by Henrietta Louise Swanson?

MICHAEL

(*impatiently*) No. I've never heard of it.

ELLIOTT

An extremely fascinating book. It's about the Chinese.

MICHAEL

I'll keep it in mind. Mr. Elliott . .

ELLIOTT

Farber. Elliott Farber.

MICHAEL

Mr. Farber, you've got the wrong man. I've never been to Jason's.

ELLIOTT

Yes, yes. I understand how embarrassing these admissions can be. I won't press the issue. Suffice it to say that you're dealing not with a fun-loving girl, but with a seriously disturbed individual who needs constant professional attention. If you care at all for her future happiness, you'll call me — I'll leave my number — the next time she drops by . . to pay a visit.

MICHAEL

There's never been a first time, but I guess nothing will convince you of that.

ELLIOTT

You're absolutely right. You see, Helene absolves herself of guilt by eventually confessing everything to me. As a consequence, I know just about

169

everything she does. (*wistfully*) It's pathetic, but there's almost something childlike about her when she relates these experiences. She's like a little girl, telling her father she accidentally broke his best pipe. (*slight pause; on the line*) I come from a very wealthy family. Money means almost nothing to me. If I have to spend my last dollar to help the girl I love, I'll do it. And those who help me I'll reward handsomely. Now I must be going. I'm sorry to have bothered you. If it was unpleasant for you, it was doubly unpleasant for me.

MICHAEL

I'm sure it was. Well, don't forget your gloves.

ELLIOTT

I couldn't do that — not in this weather. My, but it's nasty out. There's nothing quite so bone-chilling as a cold March rain. I'm almost tempted not to go home. (*slight pause*) Are you married?

MICHAEL

Not quite.

ELLIOTT

Engaged, are you?

MICHAEL

No . .

ELLIOTT

Oh, you're getting a divorce.

MICHAEL

It's not that either. My wife . . disappeared several years ago.

ELLIOTT

I didn't mean to pry.

MICHAEL

Yes, she was in the habit of taking a morning constitutional around Farview Lake. We lived in the mountains then. One day she didn't come back. She was last seen leaning over an old wooden jetty, whistling "Greensleeves" at the water.

ELLIOTT

How sad. I wondered when I saw the double bed.

MICHAEL

I purposely kept the bed.

ELLIOTT

Well, that's a consolation. Oh, before I forget, here's my card. (*He removes a card from his wallet and hands it to Michael.*) Farber — Elliott Farber.

MICHAEL

I'll put this where I won't lose it.

ELLIOTT

It doesn't matter if you do. I'm listed. Well, I'd better not keep my chauffeur waiting any longer. Good night, Mr. McVey.

MICHAEL

Yes . . good night. (*Elliott leaves. Michael closes the door, then walks to the window. Sound of a car pulling away. He throws the card into the wastebasket and goes to the easy chair. He sits and begins to read. Slow fade to blackout. Full lights up. Afternoon. Sound of running water from offstage bathroom. Michael whistling "Greensleeves." A girl appears in the hallway. She is around 27, very attractive, and nicely dressed. There is a pleasing manner about her. She checks the number on the door and knocks several times.*)

MICHAEL'S VOICE

(*annoyed*) I'll be there in a second. (*Michael enters with some shaving cream on his face. He wipes it off with a towel before he opens the door.*)

GIRL

Hello. I'm looking for a Michael McVey.

MICHAEL

You're looking right at him.

GIRL

I see I've picked a bad time to come.

MICHAEL

You have. What can I do for you?

GIRL

I can drop by later.

MICHAEL

I won't be here later. (*slight pause*)

GIRL

My name is Helene Carlyle.

MICHAEL

Carlyle? (*short pause*) Oh, yes.

HELENE

I've come to apologize for Mr. Farber's behavior Tuesday. We had dinner together last night. He told me what happened.

MICHAEL

Fascinating, wasn't it?

HELENE

No; sad, really. He's done this several times before. It gets to be em-

171

barrassing after a while. (*She takes out a cigarette.*) I can't seem to find my lighter. Do you have a match?

MICHAEL

(*after a pause*) Not on me. But . . come in, and I'll get one. (*looks her over*) Have a seat. (*He goes into the kitchen; she sits in the easy chair. He returns with a pack of matches and lights her cigarette.*)

HELENE

Thank you. (*She inhales and exhales slowly.*) He was quite nervous during the dinner — rambled on about anything and everything. I knew something was wrong. Then he came out with these accusations . . about you and me.

MICHAEL

I take it Mr. Farber has a drinking problem.

HELENE

This has nothing to do with alcohol. You see, he's been going to an analyst. Unfortunately, it isn't doing him much good.

MICHAEL

You're Mr. Farber's fiancée?

HELENE

We're simply good friends. I've been dating him off and on for about a year. Elliott's a nice person — in spite of his eccentricities. I hope you weren't offended.

MICHAEL

I don't offend easily. I was puzzled more than anything else. How did he happen to pick me?

HELENE

I honestly can't answer that. He refuses to tell me. You're not connected with the opera, by any chance?

MICHAEL

No, but I go — occasionally.

HELENE

He could have met you there. He meets a lot of people at the opera. Maybe he spoke to you during an intermission. Elliott never forgets a name or a face.

MICHAEL

I never talk with strangers, and I don't remember meeting anyone during an intermission.

HELENE

A mutual friend, perhaps?

MICHAEL

I doubt it.

HELENE

Well, there's always the telephone directory. (*She laughs a little.*) I can picture him poring over the pages — looking for a likely candidate. I shouldn't laugh; it isn't funny. The man needs to be helped.

MICHAEL

Mr. Farber told me he's wealthy. A man with his money shouldn't find it hard . . to get help.

HELENE

Oh, Elliott's receiving excellent psychiatric treatment. The catch is, he refuses to talk about himself to the doctor. He claims his visits are strictly for my benefit. Elliott tells the doctor I'm so ashamed of my actions that I requested a third party — him — to speak for me.

MICHAEL

Have him see another psychiatrist.

HELENE

Elliott wouldn't hear of it. He and the doctor are the best of friends. But that's what Elliott says. What Dr. Sasser says . .

MICHAEL

Dr. Sasser?

HELENE

Yes; do you know him?

MICHAEL

No, but I've heard about him.

HELENE

Oh? Where?

MICHAEL

Uh . . in some psychiatric journal I found lying around the office.

HELENE

That's interesting. Where is your office?

MICHAEL

(*after a pause*) In the city.

HELENE

What kind of work do you do?

MICHAEL

Uninteresting work.

HELENE

I guess you don't especially like what you're doing.

173

MICHAEL

I'm thinking about changing jobs.

HELENE

I can sympathize with you. I've just changed jobs myself. What was I saying? Oh, yes. Dr. Sasser. Well, Elliott wouldn't trade him for the world. They even go to the opera together. From what I understand, it's part of the therapy.

MICHAEL

(*weak smile*) Does Sasser bring along a folding couch, or does Farber lie down in the aisle between acts?

HELENE

I don't know. I never asked. The whole thing is probably Elliott's idea; he always buys the tickets. They haven't missed an opening night this year.

MICHAEL

Opening nights are more therapeutic?

HELENE

No, just more expensive. Elliott's paid some outlandish prices for tickets. He's rather free with his money, to say the least.

MICHAEL

Is that why you date him?

HELENE

Pardon?

MICHAEL

I said, is that why . .

HELENE

(*interrupting*) I heard what you said. And the answer is Yes . . and No. Yes, because . . he's generous — I hope that doesn't sound too mercenary — and No, because I honestly enjoy his company. Most of the time, that is. Oh, he gets tiresome now and then, but on the whole he can be entertaining. He's traveled widely, knows hundreds of people. Important people, too. (*Michael regards her for a moment.*)

MICHAEL

Would you like a drink? I should have offered you something before.

HELENE

That sounds nice. I can't stay too long, though.

MICHAEL

What'll it be?

HELENE

Well, I'd be lying if I said I was impartial to wine.

MICHAEL

I have some claret.

HELENE

I see we have similar tastes. A small glass, please.

MICHAEL

Take off your coat. I'll only be a second. (*Michael goes into the kitchenette. Helene walks about the room. He returns with a glass of wine.*) Here you are.

HELENE

Hmmm. Thank you. Aren't you having any?

MICHAEL

I never drink before six — not even wine. More habit than anything else.

HELENE

You save your pleasures for sundown, is that it?

MICHAEL

Not all my pleasures.

HELENE

Only some. Well, "Kan-pai." (*She sips.*) That's Japanese for "bottoms up." I used to date a foreign exchange student in college.

MICHAEL

So did I.

HELENE

Japanese?

MICHAEL

Nepalese.

HELENE

I've never been to Nepal.

MICHAEL

Neither have I. I don't think many people have.

HELENE

(*sipping wine*) I must say this is relaxing. I was expecting an angry emotional outburst from the injured party. It's refreshing to meet someone so understanding.

MICHAEL

I was angry . . when it happened. But now I'm almost glad it did.

HELENE

How do you mean?

MICHAEL

This meeting.

175

HELENE

Come now, does your wife know how you drop your compliments?

MICHAEL

I'm not married.

HELENE

I thought Elliott told me you were. (*walks toward the window*) Can you tell me what that building is across the street? The odd-looking one — with the large windows. I didn't see a sign or anything.

MICHAEL

It doesn't have one. For some reason the owner didn't think it was important to put one up. It's an oriental dance studio, run by a recent émigré from Mongolia. Modern dance and ballet, I hear.

HELENE

An oriental dance studio? How strange. I never knew such a thing existed in this part of the city.

MICHAEL

I never knew myself until . . someone told me. Hardly anyone ever leaves or enters the building — not through the front entrance, anyway. There must be a way of getting in through the back.

HELENE

I wonder if any Westerners study there.

MICHAEL

Westerners?

HELENE

You know, occidentals.

MICHAEL

I haven't seen any.

HELENE

But there's no real way of knowing . . if there's a rear entrance.

MICHAEL

That's true. (*slight pause*) What do you plan to do if Farber doesn't get well? Will you still see him?

HELENE

I haven't decided. It never occurred to me that he might not. When Elliott's with me he acts so normal. These accusations come so infrequently; and when they do, I'm tempted to regard them as simply — lapses into bad taste.

MICHAEL

Who were some of the other people he's accused?

HELENE

The one before you was a married man with three children — no, four. He was very upset by the whole affair and threatened to sue, but Elliott's doctor arranged some kind of financial settlement. And then there was a young Roman Catholic priest — a Father Finley, from St. James parish. He knew Elliott was sick and tried his best to help him. But Elliott was so insistent with his charges that the priest had to notify his bishop. Well, one thing led to another, and before it was all over, the priest suffered a complete nervous breakdown.

MICHAEL

Why do you think he does it? Jealousy?

HELENE

I wouldn't even begin to guess. There is no reason for him to be jealous. He understands our relationship perfectly.

MICHAEL

Hhmmm. Would you care for another glass?

HELENE

But I've barely touched this one.

MICHAEL

Some people like to drink from two glasses.

HELENE

Do they? I've never heard of that. (*slight pause*) This will be fine.

MICHAEL

(*observes her*) Tell me, do you only date Mr. Farber?

HELENE

At present, yes.

MICHAEL

Any particular reason?

HELENE

Time, mostly. In addition to my regular job, I play with the city symphony. Lately we've been fairly busy with rehearsals and engagements.

MICHAEL

Uh . . clavichord, right?

HELENE

Wrong. French horn. I did play the clavichord, but gave it up about five years ago.

MICHAEL

I'd like to hear you play.

HELENE

The clavichord?

177

MICHAEL
No, the French horn.

HELENE
You'll have to come to one of our concerts. The new series begins in four weeks.

MICHAEL
I don't know if I can wait four weeks.

HELENE
You enjoy music that much?

MICHAEL
Much more than you could imagine.

HELENE
I should have known you were a music fan when I saw your parakeet. Most music lovers keep birds.

MICHAEL
It's not a parakeet; it's a myna bird.

HELENE
I didn't get a close look. Myna birds talk, don't they?

MICHAEL
They imitate sounds, yes.

HELENE
Does your bird talk?

MICHAEL
He says a few things.

HELENE
Like what?

MICHAEL
Numbers, mostly. One-two-three, one-two-three. Nothing very involved.

HELENE
Perhaps you should talk to it.

MICHAEL
I tried that, but I felt silly talking to a bird. Do you have a bird?

HELENE
No, I don't have a bird.

MICHAEL
Did you ever have one?

HELENE
No, I never had one.

MICHAEL
You never had a bird? Now what kind of music lover are you? (*She crosses*

her left leg over her right leg. She sips the wine and stares at him.) I said
. . what kind of music lover are you? (*She crosses her right leg over her
left leg. She sips and stares.*) I said . . what kind of . . music lover . .
are you? (*Fade to half light. Tableau. Fade to blackout. Fade up on room.
Early evening. Michael is alone, pacing back and forth, nervously smoking a cigarette. He puts it out and goes to the kitchenette, returns with two
glasses and fills them with wine. He sits in the easy chair and sips slowly
from both. He hums "Greensleeves" erratically, then walks to the window
— pausing momentarily in front of the telephone. He begins to pick up the
opera glasses, but instead goes to the telephone directory and flips rapidly
through it. He picks up the phone and dials. Pause.*)

May I speak with Mr. Farber, please? (*listens*) Elliott Farber. (*listens*)
I'll wait. (*pause*) Hello, Mr. Farber? This is Mr. McVey. Michael McVey.
You . . visited me last week. (*listens*) Very well, thank you. I was wondering if you could drop by my apartment later on this evening. I have
something to tell you. (*listens*) I'd rather not. It might be best if I spoke
to you in person. (*Listens. Checks his watch.*) Five thirty. (*listens*) Yes,
I'll be in all night. Seven o'clock? See you at seven. (*listens*) As I said, I'd
rather not. It's about Helene. She's been here . . again. (*Slow fade to
blackout. Full light on room. Evening. Elliott enters the room carrying a
white Angora cat under his left arm. He is smiling broadly.*)

ELLIOTT

Well, well, well. So nice to see you again. What a *surprise* it was to hear
your voice. For a moment I couldn't imagine . .

MICHAEL

Here, I'll take your coat.

ELLIOTT

Yes, it is a bit warm in here; but it's a blessing to get out of that dampness.

MICHAEL

I'll open a window.

ELLIOTT

No, don't do that. Dido, here, is affected by drafts. (*to the cat*) Say hello
to Mr. McVey, Dido. (*slight pause*) She's bashful in front of strangers.

MICHAEL

Well, won't you have a seat. (*Elliott sits on the sofa. The cat is in his lap.*)

ELLIOTT

Terrible weather we're having, isn't it. Rain, rain, all the time rain. Sometimes I wonder why I stay north this time of year. Mother was saying at
dinner tonight that she simply can't recall a spring so nasty. If it wasn't for
the opera, you know, I could never tolerate this dreary city.

179

MICHAEL

Can I get you a drink?

ELLIOTT

That's very kind of you, but I'm absolutely bursting. We had braised mandarin duck with water chestnuts and tangerine sauce for dinner, and I'm ashamed to say I've made a pig of myself. I positively go insane over water chestnuts.

MICHAEL

The reason why I called was . .

ELLIOTT

You don't know how much of a godsend your phone call was. Shortly before you rang, Goodwin — he's my brother — Goodwin was trying to embroil me in a debate about Burmese economics. Now I'm not the least bit interested in how the Burmese spend their money. But that's one fact among many that I've been unable to communicate to Goodwin. There's no talking to him ever since he discovered the Pali alphabet and learned Sino-Tibetan. (*short pause*) You were saying?

MICHAEL

I was saying the reason I called was to tell you that . . Helene dropped by this afternoon.

ELLIOTT

Is that so? We had dinner together last night. She told me she planned to spend Sunday afternoon practicing her instrument.

MICHAEL

She spent the afternoon here.

ELLIOTT

Practicing her instrument?

MICHAEL

Uh . . no.

ELLIOTT

Now obviously she's lied to me. I wonder why she did that? (*to the cat*) What's the matter, Dido? She's restless. I think she misses Maxine. Maxine is her sister. Her twin sister. (*to the cat*) Do you miss your sister? Hmmmm? (*to Michael*) Maxine is at home with a . . how shall I say it? . . tummy ache. But we don't talk about *that*, do we, Dido? *No we don't.* (*to Michael*) I'm sorry; go on.

MICHAEL

Yes, Helene came by around two o'clock. Acted as though she had never been here before. Affected surprise at almost everything. Pretended not to know me. I went along with her, figured it was some kind of delusion.

ELLIOTT

You were wise to do that. She's gone into these trances twice before. (*to the cat*) What *is* it, Dido? Do you mind if I put her on the bed? She's very good that way. (*He puts the cat on the bed and returns to the couch.*) Angoras are so temperamental. Dido and Maxine were only kittens when I picked them up in Hong Kong three summers ago. They've grown so. (*wistfully*) I hardly know them anymore. (*slight pause*) Now back to Helene.

MICHAEL

She acted strange, unusual. Had me worried for a while. Then I remembered what you said about her — that she was emotionally disturbed. I offered some wine, thinking it might snap her back. She only wanted more. After the fourth glass I cut her off. She complained about the room being too hot. I started to open a window, but she said she was afraid of getting a chill. That's when she began to . .

ELLIOTT

(*angrily, to the cat*) Sit, Dido! Sit and be good! I don't understand these cats anymore. She's going to turn out exactly like Maxine. Wants to run outside the first chance she gets. God knows why! She has her satin pillows, her salmon steaks, her mahogany litter box. What more could she want? (*slight pause; smiles, pleasantly*) I've interrupted you again.

MICHAEL

There's not much more to say except that . . well, she's becoming . . indecent. Suggested things that would shock a sailor.

ELLIOTT

For instance.

MICHAEL

There's no need to go into details. Give your imagination free rein.

ELLIOTT

I see. Her condition appears to be worsening. That's unfortunate, too. She was making progress.

MICHAEL

Has she seen a doctor?

ELLIOTT

She refuses to go.

MICHAEL

Can't you make her?

ELLIOTT

Make her? (*slight pause*) I've tried so many times, but she's so overwhelmed with a sense of guilt that . . facing a doctor is completely out of

181

the question for her. (*fondly*) Look — Dido likes your bed. (*to the cat*) Do you like Mr. McVey's bed, Dido? She's such a good cat. I'm sorry I yelled at her like that. Maxine is the one who should be yelled at.

MICHAEL

Are you going to tell Helene I called?

ELLIOTT

Do you think I should?

MICHAEL

You know what's best.

ELLIOTT

Offhand, I'd say it might be a bad thing if I did. One never knows how she'll react. (*slight pause*) No, definitely not. She'd probably get hysterical.

MICHAEL

Then what will you do?

ELLIOTT

What I've been doing for several months. I'll pass this information on to a specialist I know. He's been advising me about her.

MICHAEL

Mr. Farber, do her activities . . bother you in any way?

ELLIOTT

(*a sigh*) They do. However, I try not to let my true feelings show. It's not an easy thing.

MICHAEL

When will you see Helene again?

ELLIOTT

Saturday night. Harvey Ellis-Fermore and his wife are giving a midnight-'til-morn party in their new greenhouse. It's going to be a lavish affair. Bettina, Harvey's wife, is having three thousand baby orchids flown in from Bangkok. The Ellis-Fermores don't entertain often — but when they do! Splendid hosts, they are. I've asked Helene to come along. (*Michael begins to pet the cat.*)

MICHAEL

There's . . something else I have to tell you.

ELLIOTT

Oh?

MICHAEL

Helene made a little confession to me.

ELLIOTT

A confession? When?

182

MICHAEL
This afternoon.

ELLIOTT
Did she, now? What did she say?

MICHAEL
She told me that she doesn't love you, that she never did, that she's only seeing you for your money. (*pause*)

ELLIOTT
(*calmly*) Helene said that?

MICHAEL
She said a lot more. She was very abusive. One would never guess from her . . genteel exterior that she had such a wanton streak.

ELLIOTT
Are you certain it wasn't the wine speaking?

MICHAEL
She said all that before she even touched the wine.

ELLIOTT
Helene abusive? That's so hard to believe.

MICHAEL
She called you vile names, said you had evil habits, said you recently struck your mother at a card party.

ELLIOTT
(*little laugh*) Preposterous. Why I would never *dream* of striking my mother. She's deteriorated beyond what I imagined. The poor girl is totally demented. (*slight pause*)

MICHAEL
She said something else.

ELLIOTT
Something else?

MICHAEL
Maybe I shouldn't say it.

ELLIOTT
No, go on. Feel free. I've an open mind.

MICHAEL
Shortly before she left, she walked over to me and whispered into my ear: "I love you."

ELLIOTT
She whispered that in your ear? Was there someone else in the room?

MICHAEL
We were alone.

ELLIOTT
Then why did she whisper?

MICHAEL
It's an intimate way of saying things.

ELLIOTT
She never whispered in my ear.

MICHAEL
You've never been intimate with her?

ELLIOTT
What?

MICHAEL
What I mean is, have you ever been in a romantic situation with Helene?

ELLIOTT
Depends what you mean by romantic. I've not taken liberties, if that's
what you're implying. There's something felonious about that, isn't there
— taking advantage of a disordered person?

MICHAEL
I wasn't suggesting that at all; I . .

ELLIOTT
I know you weren't. It's my nerves. The whole affair has put such a strain
on me. (*goes to cat*) Come here, Dido. Come to Papa. (*picks up cat*) Do
you like your daddy? (*to Michael*) I'm absolutely crazy about animals.
They're such a comfort, and they're so trusting — especially in times of
stress. Sometimes I don't know what I'd do without them. I'm not a man
of faith — although lately I tried my hand at Roman Catholicism. It didn't
work. A man without religion needs someone, something. That's why I
need Helene — and, of course, Dido.

MICHAEL
Mr. Farber, I'd like to propose something.

ELLIOTT
Please do. But let's not have any more Mr. Farbers — or Mr. McVeys.

MICHAEL
Elliott, why not have Helene committed?

ELLIOTT
Helene — committed? To what, an institution?

MICHAEL
A home. A rest home.

ELLIOTT
That's the same as an institution.

184

MICHAEL

You could send her to one of the better ones in the country. They're not like homes at all; they're like resorts, with acres of rose bushes and rolling greens. She'd live in a home resembling an antebellum plantation house — tall, white pillars, huge porticos. And nobody there wears a uniform.

ELLIOTT

You've seen these places?

MICHAEL

Only in documentaries.

ELLIOTT

I never knew they existed.

MICHAEL

Not many people do.

ELLIOTT

Helene really does need a change away from the city. It's getting to be too much for her. City life can be trying — even for a normal person.

MICHAEL

It's only a suggestion.

ELLIOTT

Yes, a rest; that's definitely what she needs. Are these country homes mixed?

MICHAEL

Mixed?

ELLIOTT

Coeducational. Men and women sharing the same facilities.

MICHAEL

Most of them are. Everything is done to approximate everyday living conditions.

ELLIOTT

Hmmm. But considering the nature of her disturbance, do you feel it's safe to send her to such a place? God forbid she should . . annoy some of the other patients.

MICHAEL

Everyone is carefully watched. Nothing like that goes on. Not in the better homes.

ELLIOTT

Good. I'm relieved to hear that. Do you have any particular place in mind?

MICHAEL

As I said, my knowledge is only secondhand.

ELLIOTT

No great problem. I know someone who can recommend one. This is such an excellent idea, I'm sorry I didn't think of it myself. You can't begin to realize how grateful I am for your interest. Helene means a good deal to me.

MICHAEL

I do what I can to help people.

ELLIOTT

I know that, Michael, and that's why I want to do something nice for you. When I return home, the very first thing I'm going to do is sit down and write a very generous check in your name.

MICHAEL

Mr. Farber . .

ELLIOTT

Elliott.

MICHAEL

Elliott, that isn't why I volunteered this information.

ELLIOTT

Obviously not.

MICHAEL

Helene means as much to me as she does to you — in a different way, of course. You love her, I like her. But that's not to say I'd do anything less to help her.

ELLIOTT

Don't say another word. It's clear you have her well-being at heart. Nevertheless, I won't be deterred from expressing my gratitude to you. I'll mail the check in the morning.

MICHAEL

Elliott . .

ELLIOTT

Now not another word! I must be off. A friend and I are going to hear *Madame Butterfly* tonight and I don't want to be late. I hope it stopped raining. (*He goes to window.*) It's getting worse instead of better. I wouldn't have to worry about the weather in Miami. But, sad to say, Miami doesn't have the opera. (*He stops at the birdcage.*) Look, Dido, a little bird. What's his name?

MICHAEL

He doesn't have one. I haven't gotten around to naming him yet.

ELLIOTT

Just get him?

MICHAEL
No, I've had him for a while.

ELLIOTT
He should be named. I've discovered that animals are unusually sensitive to names — isn't that right, Dido? I wonder what would happen if I put Dido into the cage?

MICHAEL
That might not work.

ELLIOTT
No, ha, ha, I don't suppose it would. Forgive me; I was only being devilish. (*checks watch*) I've got to run. Again, a million thanks for everything.

MICHAEL
Don't say another word.

ELLIOTT
Aha . . not another word. Say goodnight to Michael, Dido. (*slight pause*) She's bashful in front of strangers. (*Blackout. Full light up only in hallway. The room is in complete darkness except for a small amount of light coming through the windows. Barely discernible is the inert figure of Michael sleeping in bed. He makes soft, fitful sounds. Suddenly Helene appears in the hall. She is wearing a full-length white ermine coat. She knocks softly on the door several times.*)

MICHAEL
What? Is someone there? (*She knocks again. He gets up and turns on the floor lamp. He puts on a robe, checks the clock, and stands near the door.*) Who is it?

HELENE
It's me; may I come in?

MICHAEL
Who are you?

HELENE
Helene. Let me in. (*He opens the door.*)

MICHAEL
What is this . . ?

HELENE
I had to see you. I'm sorry.

MICHAEL
Do you know what time it is?

HELENE
(*checks her watch*) It's exactly four o'clock.

187

MICHAEL

You normally get people out of bed at four?

HELENE

Of course not. This is the first time I've done it.

MICHAEL

I don't think it's right for you to be here.

HELENE

I don't see why not.

MICHAEL

He might think otherwise.

HELENE

He? Do you mean Elliott?

MICHAEL

Why provoke him. Can't you see me in the morning?

HELENE

It is morning.

MICHAEL

Late morning.

HELENE

No.

MICHAEL

I have a phone, you know.

HELENE

It's unlisted.

MICHAEL

So it is. Well, what do you want?

HELENE

Some wine would be nice.

MICHAEL

You're not serious.

HELENE

Oh, but I am. I told you, I adore wine.

MICHAEL

And I adore sleep.

HELENE

You're not being especially cordial.

MICHAEL

Well, I'm odd that way. I have this thing about people waking me at four
A.M.

HELENE

Do you like my coat?

MICHAEL

It's lovely.

HELENE

Ermine. Elliott bought it for me.

MICHAEL

Is this how you spend your twilight hours — showing off your furs?

HELENE

What an appealing sense of humor you have. I'd like some wine, please. (*He goes to the kitchenette. Helene takes a lighter from her purse and lights a cigarette. Michael returns with the wine.*)

MICHAEL

All right — what is it?

HELENE

"Kan-pai." (*She sips.*) Elliott bores me.

MICHAEL

How interesting.

HELENE

He bores me to death. Sometimes I get so that I simply can't stand him.

MICHAEL

Don't see him anymore.

HELENE

I'd like not to, but I feel morally obligated.

MICHAEL

Elliott says you don't have any morals.

HELENE

Elliott is a sick man.

MICHAEL

I thought you were going to a party tonight.

HELENE

I went, but couldn't stay.

MICHAEL

Where's Elliott?

HELENE

Oh, he's still there. When I left, he and old Ellis-Fermore were in the middle of a deep discussion about Asian economics. I told him I had a headache from all those orchids. He had a taxi come for me.

MICHAEL

And instead of going home, you came here.

HELENE
Not exactly. I went home first.

MICHAEL
Said hello to Mom and Dad, huh?

HELENE
I've come here on serious business.

MICHAEL
A minute ago you said you came because you were bored.

HELENE
Boredom can be serious business. But it's more than boredom. It's concern.

MICHAEL
For whom?

HELENE
For Elliott. He's going over the deep end.

MICHAEL
Really?

HELENE
Dr. Sasser called me the other day. He claims Elliott's stories are becoming more frequent and more fantastic. The doctor feels he's on the verge of a breakdown.

MICHAEL
Why come here and tell me?

HELENE
Because I need your help.

MICHAEL
My help? We're practically . . complete strangers.

HELENE
That's true, yet somehow I feel we have a lot in common.

MICHAEL
Somehow I don't.

HELENE
I could refuse to see Elliott again and that would solve my problem. For Elliott it would be a different story.

MICHAEL
I don't understand why you'd have any second thoughts about not seeing him. After all, you are only friends.

HELENE
It's not as simple as that. I've incurred obligations.

MICHAEL
(*pointing to the fur*) Give the obligations back.

HELENE
I wasn't referring to his gifts.

MICHAEL
What else is there?

HELENE
I don't know. It's hard to express. Something intangible . . like an emotional commitment. Once you get involved, you don't easily break away.

MICHAEL
Who told you that, Dr. Sasser? It sounds like a line from one of his articles.

HELENE
As a matter of fact, he intimated something to that effect.

MICHAEL
Exactly what kind of help do you want?

HELENE
Dr. Sasser thinks Elliott should be put away for a while.

MICHAEL
Away?

HELENE
In a home. A rest home.

MICHAEL
A country rest home?

HELENE
Something similar to that. The doctor made inquiries about having Elliott committed to one of those plush, private homes upstate. However, the Farber family was totally opposed to the idea. They're concerned about a scandal. They have their position to protect.

MICHAEL
They'll have a lot more to protect if he keeps up what he's doing.

HELENE
The Farbers realize that, so they've agreed to Sasser's second proposal.

MICHAEL
Which is?

HELENE
Elliott has been talking for some time now about taking a trip to the Far East. He's asked me to join him several times, but I've never given him a definite answer. Sasser thinks I should agree to go. The doctor has a friend who runs a small mental-health clinic on Formosa — in Tainan. If I can

get Elliott there, Sasser will take care of the rest. It will only be a matter of signing a few papers.

MICHAEL

And what do you get out of this?

HELENE

(*after a pause*) Money.

MICHAEL

How much?

HELENE

(*not coy*) Enough.

MICHAEL

I don't see how I fit in.

HELENE

Elliott carries large sums with him. He never travels without protective escort.

MICHAEL

What makes you think Elliott would want me? Better yet, why do *you* want me to come along?

HELENE

Elliott thinks highly of you. He really does. He's mentioned you a few times. Said you were the only one of my "illicit" friends he approved of. I've heard nothing but compliments about you.

MICHAEL

That still doesn't prove anything.

HELENE

He seems convinced you're through with me — whatever that means. Only last night he said something about my having to look elsewhere for recreation. (*slight pause*) As for my reasons — well, as I said, Elliott bores me.

MICHAEL

Suppose I agree. I just couldn't pack up and leave.

HELENE

Why couldn't you? It will only be for a few weeks.

MICHAEL

For one thing, I have a job to worry about.

HELENE

No you don't. You're unemployed.

MICHAEL

Who told you that?

HELENE

You did.

MICHAEL

I said I was considering changing jobs.

HELENE

My error — sorry. (*pause*)

MICHAEL

I need time to think. When do you have to know?

HELENE

As soon as possible.

MICHAEL

How soon?

HELENE

Within the next few days. (*pause*)

MICHAEL

I shouldn't get involved.

HELENE

It's up to you. That's your decision. (*Pause. She walks to the window.*) That building across the street; the dance studio.

MICHAEL

What about it?

HELENE

The lights are on. I can see people moving around. You don't suppose they're dancing?

MICHAEL

It is a *dance* studio.

HELENE

Oh, but they can't be holding classes this early.

MICHAEL

Those people are probably part of a cleaning staff.

HELENE

Probably. But if they are, they're quite an agile group. Those bodies are moving fairly rapidly.

MICHAEL

Maybe they're waxing the floor.

HELENE

I wonder if they're wondering what's going on over here.

MICHAEL

There's a possibility.

HELENE

Have you come to any kind of decision?

MICHAEL

No. I'll get in touch with you.

HELENE

Why don't I contact you instead. Elliott has a habit of dropping in on me unexpectedly.

MICHAEL

Give me around three days.

HELENE

Two days sounds better.

MICHAEL

All right. Two days.

HELENE

You know something. Those people over there *are* dancing. I'm convinced of it. By the way their bodies are moving. The motion is rhythmic. (*He joins her at the window.*)

MICHAEL

It's impossible to tell from here. All you can see are blurs.

HELENE

How curious.

MICHAEL

If you're that eager to find out, you can take a look through my opera glasses. They're around here somewhere. (*Michael looks on the mantel, then goes to the bureau and searches several drawers.*)

HELENE

Michael?

MICHAEL

I found them.

HELENE

(*moving toward bed*) Michael . . the studio's lights just went out. (*Blackout. Full light up. Early evening. Elliott is sitting on the couch, looking through his billfold. Michael is packing his suitcase.*)

ELLIOTT

I know I have it written down here somewhere. (*takes out a slip of paper*) Yes, here it is. (*a beat*) We leave Kennedy at ten forty-five, stop at San Francisco around twelve forty-five A.M., their time; refuel in Honolulu some five hours later, and for the next ten hours we'll be airborne until we reach Yokohama. (*a beat*) By the way, there'll be a brief layover in Japan.

MICHAEL

(*vaguely*) Oh?

ELLIOTT

Yes, I decided it wouldn't be quite . . humane to put her away without some kind of entertainment beforehand. I thought it might be nice if we all took in a few sights before proceeding to . . (*a sigh*) to Tainan. We'll be staying at the Yokohama Hilton for three or four days — separate suites, of course. It'll be a good opportunity to get in some needed shopping. I've been promising Helene a jade bracelet for years. A friend of mine told me about this marvelous little shop on the outskirts of the city that deals exclusively in precious stones. I'm hoping to pick up a ring for myself. (*slight pause*) I really love wearing jade. It makes me feel so (*little laugh*) . . well, *jaded*. (*quickly, seriously*) I shouldn't have said that. This isn't exactly the ideal time or place for . . lightheartedness, is it? (*Michael shakes his head.*) I understand this shop carries a beautiful line of hand-crafted cuff links. Why don't you let me buy you a pair?

MICHAEL

Uh . . no. I don't wear . . cuff links.

ELLIOTT

You really should. They add so much to your wardrobe.

MICHAEL

Thanks, anyway.

ELLIOTT

Ever since Helene became ill, presenting friends with gifts has been one of the few genuine pleasures of my life. (*slight pause*) I'll get an extra pair — just in case you change your mind. (*a beat*) Is anything the matter? You seem rather subdued.

MICHAEL

I have a headache.

ELLIOTT

Take an aspirin.

MICHAEL

I've taken two. They don't seem to help.

ELLIOTT

Perhaps it's constipation. Well, don't worry about it. I'm sure it will go away. (*a beat*) Now, what were we talking about?

MICHAEL

(*after a pause*) Going away.

ELLIOTT

Oh, yes. Your presence will make the whole trip tolerable. It isn't a joyous task to have someone put away, even if it's only for a short time — hopefully. Helene will come out of this a much stronger person. I shudder when I recall Helene running through that greenhouse, screaming like a wild woman, singeing Bettina's orchids with her cigarette lighter.

MICHAEL

How did you explain my coming? Wasn't she surprised?

ELLIOTT

To be perfectly honest, she was. But I told her you at one time did some missionary work on the island and you were eager to get back to renew old acquaintances. I said the economics of my proposal appealed to you.

MICHAEL

And when we get back to the States, I'm to have your assurance that neither you nor Helene will ever contact me again.

ELLIOTT

You have my word of honor. I can well imagine what a bother we've been to you. Regretfully, one can't control life's events. Once Helene and I are married, you'll never see or hear from us again. (*slight pause*) Unless, of course, you want to.

MICHAEL

That's fair enough. Shall we toast to it?

ELLIOTT

Splendid idea. Why don't I go down and get Helene so all three of us can celebrate.

MICHAEL

(*surprised*) Helene is here?

ELLIOTT

She's waiting in the car.

MICHAEL

You didn't tell me.

ELLIOTT

I didn't think it was important. Shall we have her up? (*slight pause*)

MICHAEL

By all means. I'll get the glasses ready. (*Elliott leaves the room. Michael goes to the kitchenette. The stage is empty for about thirty seconds. Soon Helene and Elliott arrive in the hallway. They trade enigmatic glances as they enter the room. Michael comes in with a bottle of claret and a corkscrew. All three smile.*)

HELENE

Hello, Michael. How are you?

MICHAEL

Fine. How are you?

196

HELENE

I'm fine. I hear we're having a celebration.

MICHAEL

Something like that.

HELENE

I like celebrations.

MICHAEL

So do I.

ELLIOTT

That makes three of us.

HELENE

What are we drinking?

MICHAEL

Claret.

HELENE

Wonderful.

ELLIOTT

Marvelous.

MICHAEL

Make yourselves comfortable. Take off your things. (*looks out the window*) Hmmm. I see it's starting to rain again. (*Helene removes her coat and lays it on the bed. Elliott takes off his coat and gloves and tosses them over Helene's coat. The two sit on the couch.*) Excuse me for a second. (*Michael goes into the kitchenette and returns carrying a tray with six empty wine glasses. To Elliott*) I'll open, you pour.

ELLIOTT

And we'll all drink. (*Elliott pours three glasses.*) But what have we here? Six glasses? Are we expecting another threesome? (*playfully*) Perhaps I've counted wrong. (*He counts the people in the room.*) One . . two . . three. Only three. (*to Helene*) See how many you count.

HELENE

(*counts silently; smiles*) Same. Three.

ELLIOTT

It's your turn, Michael.

MICHAEL

One . . two . . three . . (*Michael takes the wine bottle from Elliott and pours three additional glasses, counting aloud as he does.*) . . four . . five . . six. (*Silence. A gong sounds softly in the distance. Silence. Blackout.*)

CURTAIN

197

The Orientals opened April 17, 1969, at the Yale School of Drama Experimental Theatre, New Haven, Conn. It was directed by Ali Taygun.

Cast of Characters

MICHAEL	David Spielberg
ELLIOTT	Michael Lombard
HELENE	Meral Taygun
DIDO	Chin Fin

DAVID KRANES

Drive-In

Cast of Characters

BOB
BOBBI
OTHER VOICES

The Setting

The skeleton of an old car, vintage early 1950's; the rest is cut away, allowing the easy throwing out of paper cups, candy wrappers, etc. It should resemble a large paint-chipped insect. A drive-in speaker hangs on the frame. It is an evening in the present.

DRIVE-IN

At the curtain: The lights dim. The sound of cartoon music begins. Throughout the cartoon music, from time to time, occurs the "beep beep" of the cartoon roadrunner. The lights come up and reveal Bob and Bobbi sitting close together, watching the cartoon, bathed in a cinematic flicker, each drinking from a paper cup. They are absorbed. A cocktail shaker sits on the floor of the car.

BOB

(*reaching down for the shaker*) Want some more?

BOBBI

Huh? . .

BOB

Want a little more?

BOBBI

Mmmm . . (*The sound of the roadrunner's "beep beep." Bobbi laughs. Bob, looking up from his pouring, laughs too. Another "beep beep." Fuller laughter from Bobbi.*)

BOB

(*handing the drink over*) Here.

BOBBI

Thanks. (*She returns to a kind of trailing, "afterthought" laughter. Bob is pouring his own drink. The sound of another "beep beep." Lighter laughter from Bobbi. The sound of cartoon windup music. The colored movie flicker fades on them momentarily, leaving them in an even, still, dim light.*)

BOB

(*looking at her, a smile*) "Beep . . beep!" (*They laugh.*) . . How are they?

BOBBI

What? . .

BOB

The drinks.

BOBBI

Mine's fine. I haven't tasted yours.

BOB

Want a taste?

BOBBI

Mmmm . . (*He gives her a taste.*) . . Same as mine.

BOB

We have the same tastes.

BOBBI

Do you like "roadrunner" cartoons? (*He tries to kiss her.*) Bob — you'll spill my drink.

BOB

Finish it. (*Music starts up. The colored flicker of light begins again.*) I'll give you three seconds to finish it.

BOBBI

I'll pass out. (*Bob makes an animal noise of mock lust.*) Stop it! . .

BOB

Put it on the floor then.

BOBBI

It might spill.

BOB

One . .

BOBBI

Bob! . .

BOB

Two . .

BOBBI

Oh — all right . . (*She sets her drink down.*)

BOB

Three! . . (*He takes her, kisses her fully. The MGM lion roars. She startles considerably. Hand to mouth*) Owww!!

BOBBI

I'm sorry.

BOB
You bit my tongue.
BOBBI
It scared me.
BOB
Jesus Christ!
BOBBI
I'm sorry, Bobby.
BOB
You're Bobbi. I'm Bob!
BOBBI
I'm sorry. Oh, look! I didn't know *he* was in it.
BOB
Who? Oh, *him*. Let me see your drink . . Shit! . . (*Eyes on screen, she reaches down, gets drink.*)
BOBBI
Oh — and look! . . (*Bob drinks. Throws the cup out the window. Pulls Bobbi over to him forcefully, kissing her. She is attempting to talk all the time he is kissing her.*) Mmghb . . orbmmmna . . tch . . brmnnaahm . .

BOB
(*breaking*) What?
BOBBI
(*pointing*) In the movie! They're watching the same cartoon on television — in the *show* — that we were watching *here*. (*A secondhand "beep beep" is heard.*)
BOB
There's lots of roadrunner cartoons.
BOBBI
No — look!
BOB
Will ya come *here*? (*They go into a kiss again, a long one. A secondhand "beep beep." The sound of a woman's and then a man's laughter. Bob and Bobbi's kiss grows more passionate.*)
MAN'S VOICE FROM THE SPEAKER
Want some more?
WOMAN'S VOICE FROM THE SPEAKER
Huh? . .
MAN'S VOICE
Want a little more?

WOMAN'S VOICE

Mmmm . . (*A secondhand "beep beep." Man's and woman's laughter: woman's fuller. Bob and Bobbi's passion grows. His hands are moving.*)

MAN'S VOICE

Here.

WOMAN'S VOICE

Thanks. (*Another secondhand "beep beep." Light woman's laughter — alone. Sound of windup cartoon music. Bob is trying to force something with Bobbi.*)

BOBBI

No! . .

BOB

Yes! . . (*The passion continues, with Bob moving Bobbi around between him and the steering wheel. From the speaker come voices again.*)

MAN'S VOICE

How is it? . . The drink.

WOMAN'S VOICE

Fine. How's yours?

MAN'S VOICE

. . I'm going to take you.

BOBBI

(*struggling*) Not in the front seat! . .

MAN'S VOICE

On the take-out counter at Howard Johnson's. (*The man and woman laugh.*)

BOBBI

(*struggling*) No! . .

WOMAN'S VOICE

. . Look — on the television — on the television, in the movie — they're watching the same cartoon we were watching. Only they're at a drive-in. (*A thirdhand "beep beep." Thirdhand laughter. Note: All thirdhand sounds and laughter and voices should be distinct and different — more staticky and removed, perhaps even with accents. Bobbi, in struggling against Bob's attempt to pin her against the steering wheel, bumps her rump against the horn. A double honk. The honk sets off a chain of car honks within the drive-in, echoing and reechoing until resolved in silence.*)

BOBBI

(*who has now repositioned herself beside Bob*) See what you did?

WOMAN'S VOICE

Robert?

MAN'S VOICE

Mmmm? . .

WOMAN'S VOICE

(*sexually*) Can you see what you're doing?

BOBBI

Bob? — I asked you a . . (*dim thirdhand "beep beep"; thirdhand laughter*)

BOB

It wasn't my ass.

THIRDHAND MAN'S VOICE

Want some more? (*accompanying thirdhand "beep beep"*)

MAN'S VOICE

Let me turn that damn television off.

WOMAN'S VOICE

(*excited*) Not now. No. Please, Robert.

BOB

Turn that speaker down — will you?

BOBBI

(*watching the film intently*) No. Not now. (*Bob tries to move in on her again.*) Not now! (*pointing at the screen*) Look!

BOB

(*persisting, playing smooth*) Bobbi . . (*Bobbi complies.*)

WOMAN'S VOICE

Robert! . .

THIRDHAND MAN'S VOICE

Roberta . .

THIRDHAND WOMAN'S VOICE

You'll spill my drink.

MAN'S VOICE

(*playfully, sexually*) You bit my tongue.

WOMAN'S VOICE

I just wanted a taste.

MAN'S VOICE

We have the same tastes.

WOMAN'S VOICE

Look at them. On the television. In their car.

MAN'S VOICE

They have nothing on us.

WOMAN'S VOICE

They have nothing on themselves.

BOBBI

Not in the front seat! . .

WOMAN'S VOICE

They've moved to the back seat.

MAN'S VOICE

Don't change the subject. Come here.

WOMAN'S VOICE

(*playful*) You're not Warren Beatty. (*Bobbi has broken and is movie-watching.*)

BOB

Come here . .

BOBBI

That's Michael Caine! . .

MAN'S VOICE

Who cares! . .

BOB

Who cares.

WOMAN'S VOICE

(*sensual, prolonged*) Mmmmm . . mmmmmm . . (*Bob has moved in on Bobbi again. She tries to break to watch the movie.*)

BOBBI

Mmmmghmmm!! . .

WOMAN'S VOICE

(*sensual*) Robert! . .

BOBBI

Bob!! . .

THIRDHAND WOMAN'S VOICE

Bert . .

THIRDHAND MAN'S VOICE

Roberta . .

BOB

Bobbi!

MAN'S VOICE

Robin! . .

BOB

Jesus! . .

WOMAN'S VOICE

Oh, God! . .

BOB

What's the matter with you tonight?!

BOBBI
I'm excited.

BOB
You'd never know it!

BOBBI
I am.

BOB
Sure.

WOMAN'S VOICE
Oh! . .

BOBBI
Watching them.

BOB
Watch yourself.

MAN'S VOICE
(*gently*) Are you all right?

WOMAN'S VOICE
Mmmm . .

BOBBI
That's what I mean. I *have* to. I get so excited. I get these feelings. And then I get frightened. I get very afraid sometimes, Bob. I worry about myself. You just don't understand. What things like this do to me.

MAN'S VOICE
Are you afraid? . .

WOMAN'S VOICE
Not any more . .

BOB
I understand . . I do.

THIRDHAND MAN'S VOICE
You bit my tongue.

MAN'S VOICE
Turn that off.

BOB
I just wish they'd turn their damned television off.

WOMAN'S VOICE
It's all right. I like to watch the light flickering on our skin. (*Bob and Bobbi become aware of the movie lights flickering on their skin.*)

MAN'S VOICE
You're wonderful . .

207

WOMAN'S VOICE

It's all right. They're in the back seat now anyway. (*The man and woman laugh lightly, gently together.*)

BOB

(*trying to be understanding*) I understand . . I do. No kidding. I mean about your being frightened and everything. There are lots of frightening things.

BOBBI

I know.

BOB

I get frightened too.

BOBBI

You do.

BOB

Sure.

BOBBI

I wouldn't ever have thought that.

BOB

I do. I keep a hunting pistol in the glove compartment there. Just in case. Mostly I just shoot rats at the dump, but you never know. You never know what's going to happen.

BOBBI

That's not exactly what I meant. (*the sound of the ocean*)

BOB

But you never know.

BOBBI

(*pointing to the screen*) Look — it's the next day. I bet he stayed there. With her. They're walking. It looks something like Montauk. They film things at Montauk. I wonder if it is. They really love each other.

BOB

Are you still excited?

BOBBI

Very.

BOB

Are you still afraid?

BOBBI

Not so much.

BOB

Do you want another drink?

BOBBI

No — thank you . . Do you love me, Bob? I mean, really?

BOB

Sure.

BOBBI

. . good. (*They begin their passion again. The sound of surf breaking in. The sound builds with their passion.*)

MAN'S VOICE

. . You seem distant today.

WOMAN'S VOICE

I'm sorry.

MAN'S VOICE

Something the matter?

WOMAN'S VOICE

Things change — that's all. I'm just thinking that things change.

MAN'S VOICE

You mean us? (*Bob and Bobbi are nearly standing on the car seat now, beginning to work their way — without unclinching — over the front seat and into the back.*)

WOMAN'S VOICE

. . Smell the salt!

MAN'S VOICE

Watch out — you'll get wet.

WOMAN'S VOICE

I don't care. Look. Robert. Look at that gull there. It's so alone. It must be a woman gull.

MAN'S VOICE

Why do you say that? (*Bob and Bobbi drop out of sight over into the back seat.*)

WOMAN'S VOICE

There. She's gone. You can't see her any more.

MAN'S VOICE

Or him. (*Light laughter. The background music gets stronger. The ocean sounds fade.*)

MAN'S VOICE

Are you cold?

WOMAN'S VOICE

Partly.

MAN'S VOICE

Would you like my sweater? (*A hand reaches up from the back seat of the car, dropping Bobbi's sweater over into the front.*)

WOMAN'S VOICE

Thank you.

MAN'S VOICE

You're shivering. How about my coat? (*The same hand from the back seat. Same action: a bra.*)

WOMAN'S VOICE

Thank you. You make me . . warm. Did you know they're going to build a drive-in on this beach? It's true. They come in on Monday to bulldoze the dunes. I'll probably cry when I see that. I think it's a shame. I always think of this as my beach. I'll feel a bit raped.

MAN'S VOICE

Figuratively speaking.

WOMAN'S VOICE

I suppose. I don't like things filling up, though. Paper cups and . . filth all over. It scares me. How do I know some ticket taker won't skip over during the cartoon and take me? I bought a gun.

MAN'S VOICE

You're kidding.

WOMAN'S VOICE

No — I did. If you'd stay with me, it would be something else. But I know better than that. I'm alone. It's just a small one.

MAN'S VOICE

Let's go back to the house. (*Sound-track music. Sound of gulls in the sky. Both sounds end, replaced by a different music, different tempo. Bob rises to sight wearily, hair mussed, shirt twisted, tapping a cigarette on his knuckles, looking over the seatback toward the screen.*)

BOB

They're back in the beach house . . Watching television again. (*third-hand "beep beep"*) . . Another roadrunner cartoon . . Something's gone wrong. I mean with them.

BOBBI'S VOICE

Where's **my bra?**

BOB

Oh — here . . (*He picks it off the front seat, hands it back.*) They're act-ing funny with each other. She's mixing drinks, cutting some cheese — and he's watching television. But you can tell there's some problem.

DRIVE-IN

BOBBI'S VOICE

My bra feels cold. Is the heater on?

BOB

(*who has returned to the front seat*) No. The roadrunner cartoon's ended.
On their television. Ha! — now the same damn movie's on.

MAN'S VOICE

The same damn movie's on.

WOMAN'S VOICE

They're all the same.

BOBBI'S VOICE

. . They're all the same.

BOB

You some kind of movie expert?

MAN'S VOICE

He's mixing her the same bloody drinks he mixed her last night. Except I
think now there's a problem. When did you get this colored set?

THIRDHAND MAN'S VOICE

Want a little more?

THIRDHAND WOMAN'S VOICE

I think we've both had enough.

MAN'S VOICE

There's a problem!

BOB

There's a problem *in* the problem!

MAN'S VOICE

I wish you'd stop fiddling around and come over here.

WOMAN'S VOICE

I'm fiddling around for you — because I thought you loved me.

BOBBI'S VOICE

Did you hear that, Bob-honey?

BOB

You say something?

BOBBI'S VOICE

No — her.

BOB

Oh . . Yeah . . Here's your sweater. (*He tosses it back.*)

BOBBI'S VOICE

I meant women do things because they think men love them.

BOB

(*pointing to the screen*) They've got problems.

211

WOMAN'S VOICE

Do you love me? Really?

MAN'S VOICE

. . Of course.

BOBBI

(*rising to sight in the back seat*) Do you love me, Bob?

BOB

(*tossing wrapper out of car*) Yeah — sure.

THIRDHAND WOMAN'S VOICE

Bert? . .

THIRDHAND MAN'S VOICE

Mmmm?

THIRDHAND WOMAN'S VOICE

Do you love me?

THIRDHAND MAN'S VOICE

Would I be here? Now? If I didn't?

BOB

. . Same damn TV show.

THIRDHAND WOMAN'S VOICE

I don't believe you.

WOMAN'S VOICE

I don't believe you.

BOBBI

I don't believe you. (*An unnaturally long silence. The next three responses are in rapid-fire overlap, almost in unison.*)

BOB

(*tossing something out; note: this pattern continues until the end of the play*) It's not my fault.

MAN'S VOICE

That's not my fault.

THIRDHAND MAN'S VOICE

That's not my fault. (*another long silence*)

WOMAN'S VOICE

Loneliness doesn't mean anything to you. It's a word. I could go to sleep night after night alone and wake up the same way and tell you and you would say, "Poor Robin! You shouldn't have to do that," and then you'd come and spend maybe two nights here — two nights, thinking all the while how good you were being to "Poor Robin. Poor, lonely Robin — all alone in that beach house, sitting there, sipping her rosé, listening to the strike and rake of waves along her beach. Looking out at the drive-in that will be up here in a couple of months . . The screen right down there. (*points*) Seeing lovers touching on the screen, walking on the screen, undressing on the screen, sleeping together on the screen. Poor Robin — alone, seeing it all through the thermoglass panes of her little house, across the sand, across the butter smells and the root-beer carbonation seeping through all the scarred convertible roofs, drifting up into the night — Poor Robin." And who are you good to in the city, Robert? Who are you good to there — for two or three nights? And how many? You sweet thing.

MAN'S VOICE

Why are you accusing me of all this?

THIRDHAND MAN'S VOICE

Why are you accusing me of all this?

BOB

What do you mean?

BOBBI

— I didn't say anything.

WOMAN'S VOICE

"Poor Robin!" Maybe I'll sneak out at night to the drive-in. Wouldn't that be something?! Peek into the steamed-up cars just to be closer to it all? (*Both Bob and Bobbi cast side glances at their respective windows.*)

MAN'S VOICE

You're overdramatizing.

BOBBI

People *know*!

BOB

No, they don't.

BOBBI

Yes, they do. I'm just cheap.

WOMAN'S VOICE

Overdramatizing?

BOB

You're not cheap.

MAN'S VOICE

Yes!

BOBBI

I *am*. Cheap and stupid.

WOMAN'S VOICE

Am I?

BOB

Don't be stupid.

THIRDHAND MAN'S VOICE
What's that?

THIRDHAND WOMAN'S VOICE
I got it to protect myself. I got it because I was alone. I got it so someone wouldn't come in here and degrade me. I think that's reasonable.

MAN'S VOICE
What are you doing with that?

WOMAN'S VOICE
You knew I had one.

THIRDHAND MAN'S VOICE
Put it down.

MAN'S VOICE
Put it down.

BOB
(he sees that Bobbi has taken his pistol from the glove compartment)
Hey! . .

THIRDHAND WOMAN'S VOICE
It's your fault.

WOMAN'S VOICE
It's your fault.

BOB
Put that down!

BOBBI
It's your fault.

BOB
No!! . .

MAN'S VOICE
No!! . .

THIRDHAND MAN'S VOICE
No! . . (A thirdhand pistol shot. A secondhand pistol shot. A firsthand pistol shot — Bobbi shoots Bob.)

THIRDHAND MAN'S VOICE
Don't you ever try that again.

THIRDHAND WOMAN'S VOICE
I'm sorry.

MAN'S VOICE
Don't you ever try that again.

WOMAN'S VOICE
I'm sorry.

BOBBI
(*looking down at the motionless Bob*) . . Oh, my God!! . . *(blackout)*

Drive-In by David Kranes opened on April 16, 1970, at Playhouse in the Park, Cincinnati, Ohio. It was directed by Patrick Tovati.

Cast of Characters

BOB	Bernard Wurger
BOBBI	Karen Grassle